SHORTLIST

Delhi

www.timeoutdelhi.net

Contents

Published under license from Time Out Guides Ltd
Universal House
251 Tottenham Court Road
London W1T 7AB
Tel: + 44 (0)20 7813 3000
Fax: + 44 (0)20 7813 6001
Email: guides@timeout.com
www.timeout.com

Managing Director Peter Fiennes
Editorial Manager Holly Pick

Time Out Guides is a wholly owned subsidiary of Time Out Group Ltd.

© **Time Out Group Ltd**
Chairman Tony Elliott

Time Out and the Time Out logo are trademarks of Time Out Group Ltd.

This edition first published in India in 2010 by Paprika Media
Paprika Media Pvt. Limited
Essar House, 11 K .K.Marg, Mahalaxmi, Mumbai - 400034, India

Distributed in Great Britain by Ebury Publishing
A Random House Group Company (www.randomhouse.co.uk)
Random House UK Limited Reg. No. 954009

Distributed in the US and Latin America by Publishers Group West
(1-510-809-3700)

Distributed in Canada by Publishers Group Canada (1-800-747-8147)

Distributed in India by Paprika Connect

ISBN: 978184670262-4

Printed and bound by Nectar Prints Pvt. Ltd., Mumbai, India

While every effort has been made by the author(s) and the publisher to ensure that the information contained in this guide is accurate and up to date as at the date of publication, they accept no responsibility or liability in contract, tort, negligence, breach of statutory duty or otherwise for any inconvenience, loss, damage, costs or expenses of any nature whatsoever incurred or suffered by anyone as a result of any advice or information contained in this guide (except to the extent that such liability may not be excluded or limited as a matter of law). Before travelling, it is advisable to check all information locally, including without limitation, information on transport, accommodation, shopping and eating out. Anyone using this guide is entirely responsible for their own health, well-being and belongings and care should always be exercised whilst travelling.

Time Out Delhi Shortlist

www.timeoutindia.net

EDITORIAL
Time Out Delhi

DESIGN
Partha Pratim Sharma,
Manoj Bhardwaj, Ritesh Kumar,
Sanjay Rawat

PHOTOGRAPHY
Paroma Mukherjee, Mikma Tshering
Lepcha, Shiv Ahuja, Taveeshi Singh,
Sushant Sinha, Anshika Varma,
Dhruba Dutta, Cherian Thomas,
Abhinandita Mathur

PRODUCTION
Harish Suvarna, Mangesh Salvi,
Sandeep Borkar

SALES
Nakul Puri, Vishwanath Shanbhag,
Amit Singh, Sudhesh Kumar,
Mohit Sharma

CIRCULATION
Shreesh Shingarey, Shakti Kamal

PUBLISHER & VP
Neelam Kapoor

CHAIRPERSON
Smiti Kanodia

MAP
Maps by MapMyIndia (www.mapmyindia.com)

About Time Out

Founded in 1968, Time Out has expanded from humble London beginnings
into the leading resource for those wanting to know what's happening in the
world's greatest cities. As well as our influential what's-on weeklies in London, New York and Chicago, we publish more than a dozen other listings
magazines in cities as varied as Beijing and Mumbai. The magazines established Time Out's trademark style: sharp writing, informed reviewing and
bang up-to-date inside knowledge of every scene.

Time Out made the natural leap into travel guides in the 1980s with the
City Guide series, which now extends to over 50 destinations around the
world. Written and researched by expert local writers and generously illustrated with original photography, the full-size guides cover a larger area than
our Shortlist guides and include many more venue reviews, along with additional background features and a full set of maps.

Throughout this rapid growth, the company has remained proudly independent, still owned by Tony Elliott four decades after he started Time Out
London as a single fold-out sheet of A5 paper. This independence extends
to the editorial content of all our publications, this Shortlist included. No establishment has been featured because it has advertised, and no payment
has influenced any of our reviews. And, for our critics, there's definitely no
such thing as a free lunch: all restaurants and bars are visited and reviewed
anonymously, and Time Out always picks up the bill.

For more about the company, see www.timeout.com.

crocs ™ available at :

Delhi Shortlist

The **Time Out Delhi Shortlist** is one of a new series of guides that draws on Time Out's background as a magazine publisher to keep you current with everything that's going on in town. As well as Delhi's key sights and the best of its eating, drinking and leisure options, the guide picks out the most exciting venues for Delhi's packed cultural calendar, all compiled by locally based editors and writers. It also includes chapters on topical reasons to visit the city, like the Commonwealth Games 2010 or medical tourism. Whether you're visiting for the first time in your life or for the first time this year, you'll find the Time Out Delhi Shortlist contains all you need to know in a portable and easy-to-use format.

The guide divides Delhi into eight areas, each containing listings for Sights & Museums, Eating & Drinking, Shopping, Nightlife and Arts & Leisure, and maps pinpointing their locations. At the front of the book are chapters rounding up these scenes city wide, and giving a shortlist of our overall picks. We also include itineraries for days out, plus transport and hotel information.

Our listings give phone numbers as dialled within Delhi. From abroad dial 0091, followed by 11 (Delhi's landline phone code) and then the number given. Ten-digit numbers are cell-phones, and don't require the 11.

Restaurant and bar listings come with the approximate price of a meal for two (two starters, two mains and two drinks), or a night out for two (four cocktails). Listings also mention when credit cards are accepted.

All our listings are double-checked, but places do occasionally close or change their hours and prices, so it's a good idea to call a venue before visiting.

Venues are marked on the maps using symbols numbered according to their order within the chapter and colour-coded as follows:

- ❶ Sights & Museums
- ❶ Eating & Drinking
- ❶ Shopping
- ❶ Nightlife
- ❶ Arts & Leisure

Delhi's major mosques are all centuries old, so they are coded as monuments.

Map key

	Stadium
	Auditorium
	Temple
	Church
	Gurudwara
	Hospital
	Hotel
	Bus Terminal
	Monument
	Museum

Don't Miss

Mallakhamb gymnastics at Connaught Place

The Red Fort

WHAT'S BEST

Sights & Museums

As one of the oldest continuously-occupied cities in the world, there is much to see in Delhi that isn't on the regular tourist agenda. That said, there are also many sights that every visitor to the city should see.

The seven ancient cities of Delhi were all independent fort-towns, each of which scattered the countryside with tombs, mosques and *sarais* (pilgrims' rest-stops). Modern Delhi is still full of innumerable monuments – nearly 1,200 are listed and more are not – waiting to be rambled through. Some, like the Qutab Minar (p132), are well-preserved and popular tourist sights. Others, like the Nizamuddin Dargah (p166), are

incredibly vital, crazy, crowded and brimming with fervent devotion. And some, like the Begampur Masjid (p130), are forgotten and magnificently silent.

The main attraction for first-time visitors is almost always the India Gate war memorial, which faces Rashtrapathi Bhavan (the President's Palace) up Rajpath. Several tour operators include a walk around nearby Connaught Place as well, carrying on toward India's biggest mosque, the Jama Masjid in the heart of the Old City. Organisations like INTACH (the Indian National Trust for Art and Cultural Heritage) arrange walks through Old Delhi, Mehrauli, Hauz Khas and other areas of historical

DLF PROMENADE
---VASANT KUNJ---
Nelson Mandela Road, Next to DLF Emporio

significance for those who want a closer look at the centuries. A newer monumental attraction is the Akshardham Temple (p200) on the Yamuna's east bank.

Delhi also has plenty of history indoors, thanks to its numerous museums (most of them in tragic condition). The National Museum (p93), an archive of India's vast artistic heritage, is obviously the most worthy and worth visiting, but you'll get more of a laugh and better stories from a visit to the surreal Parliament Museum (p95) or the Sulabh International Toilet Museum (p180).

Akshardham Temple

SHORTLIST

Classic Delhi photo-op
India Gate (p91)

Mughal grandeur
The Red Fort (p71)

Living tradition
Nizamuddin dargah (p166)

Forgotten empires
Begampur Masjid (p130)
Coronation Park (p60)
Tughlaqabad (p167)

Climbing a minaret
Jama Masjid (p70)

A moment of inner peace
The Bahà'i Temple (p161)

A bite of soul food
Bangla Sahib Gurudwara (p84)

Ancient artefacts
The National Museum (p93)

A taste of the village arts
Crafts Museum (p87)

Over-the-top modern temples
Akshardham Temple (p200)
Birla Mandir (p86)

A breath of fresh air
Lodhi Gardens (p92)
Garden of Five Senses (p131)

The past meets the future
Agrasen ki Baoli (p84)

Reach the *pinnacle* of *high fashion*

DLF PROMENADE exudes style and elegance. The world's finest fashion brands vie for your attention while you indulge your senses amidst exquisite surrounds. Come and experience the charms of this stunning lifestyle destination, where exclusive events, happenings and brands make every day special.

DLF PROMENADE
— VASANT KUNJ —

Andhra prawn masala at
Gunpowder

WHAT'S BEST
Eating & Drinking

If you're hungry, and like variety, you've come to the right place. Every part of this gluttonous city has something to offer, even if it's just off a food stall on wheels. You'll be able to find food from just about any country on earth, from France and Brazil to Korea and Uzbekistan, as well as any large community in India.

There is no quintessential Delhi cuisine, although there are at least two claimants for the title: the Mughlai (or Mughal's) food characteristic of the Muslim Old City, and the Punjabi cuisine brought in by refugees from Pakistan at the time of Partition. The Punjabi snack of chole-bhature (chickpea curry and puffy, fried bread) comes close to being a junkfood staple.

Most restaurants fall into fairly comfortable price brackets, with the five-stars and some stand-alones leaning more heavily on

Enjoy the next level of Hollywood and Bollywood entertainment, amidst unmatched luxury!

From *watching* to *experiencing*

Celebrities, fashion divas and anyone who delights in entertainment of the highest quality, chooses *DLF PROMENADE*. Of course a bevy of super exclusive fashion brands and select dining options, only add to your exquisite experience.

DLF PROMENADE
—— VASANT KUNJ ——

The ultimate hotspot for all the action in the city, concerts, events, food and chilling out!

The biggest and most amazing play area in a mall, FREE entry and unlimited fun!

Chicken neza kabab
at Gulati's

the wallet. For a tasting course in Indian *khana*, however, go no further than the food court of Dilli Haat where, for practically nothing, you can sample authentic preparations from across the country. South Indian restaurants, both "pure veg" like Udupi legend Saravana Bhavan (p107), and non-vegetarian like Chettinad-specialists Swagath (p143) abound in the city.

Certain parts of Delhi have become synonymous with particular types of cuisine. Mughlai food – biryani, mutton gosht, kababs and a host of other mutton dishes – are the mainstay of Muslim-dominated areas in the Old City and Nizamuddin. They're undoubtedly the foremost reason why Dilliwalas make regular visits to the Old City, irrespective of where they live. Neighbours (and long-standing rivals) Karim's and Al-Jawahar are the most famous establishments here, but the surrounding alleyways are full of streetside kababeries as well.

Most malls have an abundance of franchise food, so it's usually best to walk through smaller bazaars and markets to find unique flavours. Street food

he difference between

eating and *dining*

A chic all-day café where you can relax and enjoy great food amidst internationally acclaimed and award-nominated décor.

Smoke house DELI

t *DLF PROMENADE* a host of he dining restaurants come ogether to bring you a astronomic journey beyond ompare. Of course the orld's best fashion brands nd some of the city's best ntertainment options are ways just a step away.

DLF PROMENADE
VASANT KUNJ
Nelson Mandela Road, Next to DLF Emporio

MOCHA ART HOUSE

Mocha Art House elevates the concept of a multi-level experience with avant-garde space that fuses contemporary art, eclectic culture and wholesome food.

KAINOOSH
A beautiful synergy of culinary magic and stunning ambience, Kainoosh offers Fine Asian and European cuisine.

T.G.I. FRiDAYS

Get the news on what's happening at **DLF PROMENADE**.

Connect to www. acebook.com/dlfpromenade

For more information call the Info Desk at 011 – 4610 4466.

Grilled chicken with
black pepper at
the Yum Yum Tree

is available all over the city,
although first-time visitors will
have to watch what they ingest
so as to avoid "Delhi Belly".
Stick to bottled mineral water,
and avoid ice (unless it's made
from filtered water) and freshly-
cut vegetables washed in water.

Table manners

Most restaurants will give you
a fork and spoon, but it's never
considered impolite to eat Indian
food with your hand – your *right*
hand. There are no dress codes
for any restaurants, and at most
you will be expected to brush
your hair and smooth down
your shirt if you're going to an
upscale five-star joint. As a rule,
hotel restaurants do not allow
non-guests to enter in slippers
and shorts.

A quick way to save cash is
to ask what water is being served
at the table. Feel free to decline
imported mineral water and ask
for a local brand. Wherever you

eat in Delhi, a ten per cent tip is
quite standard, and while many
restaurants will add a service
charge of ten per cent to your
bill, it's still considerate to leave
something.

A vague ban on the sale of beef
applies across the board in Delhi,
making it generally impossible to
find a real steak or burger. Some
restaurants make do with water-
buffalo meat (wishfully referred
to as "buff"), and high-end
restaurants like Olive generally
serve imported beef.

Pubs & bars

Strictly speaking, outside of
the hotels, there is very little
difference between a restaurant
that serves alcohol and a bar.
Almost all restaurants in Delhi
are really resto-bars, with alcohol
and food on equal keel, staying
open till a little past midnight.
Some even have a small area
where patrons can dance,
throwing in the air of a nightclub

DLF PLACE
—SAKET—

Dine out in style, then indulge in shopping, movies and fun!

At DLF PLACE dining out means getting bewildered by choices – Big Chill, Hard Rock Café, TGIF, Eat-Food Lounge, Mainland China and Food Chowk – The New Home of India's Street-food and much more. Of course the fantastic fashion brands and great entertainment are always a step away.

If you haven't eaten in the Big Chill Café, you've missed out on some of the most delicious and eclectic gourmet delights in Delhi, amidst a deluge of mind-blowing retro Hollywood film posters and art.

Filled with awesome rock memorabilia in an eclectic atmosphere of great food and drinks, this world famous name is finally here for all fans of music and good times.

MAINLAND
CHINA
PRIVATE DINING

Discover the new home of India's street food.
The new home of Indian Street-food lives up to its promise with everything you can imagine under one 18,500 sq ft roof, from Nizam's to Paranthe Wali Gali to Karim's to Subway.

(or lounge bar) as well. These include several resident favourites like Olive, The Yum Yum Tree and Diva. Local markets in areas such as Defence Colony, Kailash Colony and Greater Kailash have resto-bars packed cheek-by-jowl.

Unless they also serve breakfast (like a hotel coffeeshop) most bars open around noon and stay open till midnight. Many will have happy hours until around 8pm, serving liquor at half-price or offering two drinks for the price of one. Alcohol shops (*thekas* in Hindi) open at noon as well, though the few in department stores open at 10am. Being a typical north Indian city, liquor sales are dominated by beer and whiskey, with rum running a close third. However if you're buying Indian-made liquor, which is entirely safe and can be quite good, rum is far and above the best bet.

The legal drinking age in Delhi (25 years) has been a subject of much debate. All establishments are required to have a sign saying no liquor will be served to minors, but no one really checks unless you look younger than 18.

Smoking

A public smoking ban came into effect in Delhi in 2008. This means most restaurants and bars are either non-smoking or have a separate section for smokers. Happily, the separate smokers' section, in most cases, is an open terrace and not a claustrophobic glass box with a ventilator. This is good news, at least until summer comes around.

SHORTLIST

Old Delhi gluttony
Karim's (p74)
Al-Jawahar (p74)

Wining and dining
Diva (p168)

South Indian canteen-style
Andhra Bhavan (p98)

Haute Indian food
Indian Accent (p169)

Beer with a view
Parikrama (p103)

Classic kabab rolls
Khan Chacha (p99)

An elegant night out
Olive (p152)

Breakfast dosas
Saravana Bhavan (p107)

Delhi's favourite, butter chicken
Moti Mahal (p77)

A peek at Delhi's heart
Punjabi By Nature (p140)

Dining al fresco
Lodi-The Garden Restaurant (p100)

Best for a taste of the entire country
Dilli Haat (p134)

Best for Kashmiri food
Chor Bizarre (p76)

DLF PLACE
— S A K E T —

CASUAL WEEKENDS
Marks & Spencers

SUITS THAT SUIT
Boggi

INTERNAL BLISS
Marks & Spencers

A combination of 182 fashion brands
and lots of fun at a unique destination.

BOOT HOUSE
Early Learning Centre

TANGY FASHION
Calonge

GREEN MUSIC
Apple

MISS CHECKERS
United Colors
of Benetton

LITTLE ZOO Early Learning Centre

CUFFLINKS Tie Rack

Purple Jungle in Hauz Khas Village

WHAT'S BEST

Shopping

For much of India, a trip to Delhi is an indispensable part of preparing for the big, fat Indian wedding. It's not just the textiles and jewellery that make the capital's shops so essential, though – shopping in Delhi throws everything into the mix, from rural handicrafts, street markets, and international high-street brands to high-end designers, traditional Indian bling and new experiments with kitschy, irreverent design.

Urban villages

Much of Delhi outside the Old City and British New Delhi was a cluster of villages with forests and fields between them. Still inhabited by the original residents, two of the larger villages, Shahpur

Jat and Hauz Khas (p148 and p146), have cannily transformed into shopping-villages filled with bookshops, cafés and boutiques selling art, antiques, and design products. Shahpur Jat still retains traces of agrarian life – tethered buffaloes and men sitting on *khatiyas* (cots) smoking tobacco.

State emporia

Delhi's "emporia" are showrooms run by India's state governments to represent their local arts, handicrafts, textiles, furniture and jewellery. They're a great pit-stop for souvenir seekers. The shops are all located on Baba Kharak Singh Marg (p108) as you exit west off Connaught Place. The prices are regulated and staff well informed, all accept credit cards

DLF PLACE
— S A K E T —

Discover exclusive fashion brands, great food and unlimited entertainment.

DLF PLACE is your style hub and family fun zone rolled into one. Find the best of fashion and lifestyle brands, a delightful choice of dining options, Hollywood and Bollywood blockbusters and entertainment for the whole family. It is the most happening shopping and entertainment destination in Delhi, and you'll want to visit again and again.

Categories: Shopping • Food Court • Cafes • Fine Dining • Entertainment • Cinema • Events

"Signature Jewels" by Mrs Vandana Bhargava and her "Heritage Collection" of art at the White and Yellow and Galleria VSB, Square One Mall, Saket

House of VSB is the outcome of years of committed effort by famous jewellery designer Vandana Bhargava. It signifies values, service and boldness. The House of VSB strives to preserve and promote our rich Indian heritage and her signature jewels are inspired by the wealth of the India's heritage jewels.

The increasing acceptance of machine-produced "costume" jewellery, which is strikingly similar to "real" jewellery, is due to smart marketing and affordability. As a result, our traditional precision craftsmen and artists are gradually changing occupations for survival. She fears that those magical fingers, which defined our glorious tradition, will soon be a thing of the past.

Bhargava has opened her flagship stores in Square One Mall in Saket, New Delhi under the name "White and Yellow-Signature Jewels by Vandana Bhargava" and Galleria VSB, as a humble attempt to promote and perpetuate our rich Indian heritage.

White and Yellow houses a rich collection of her designs that uses precious metals and the rarest mineral and organic gems and is created by some of the best Indian craftsmen under her direct supervision. The designer adds that it is virtually impossible to replicate these creations – existing craftsmen cannot achieve even 30% similarity.

What makes her signature jewels exclusive and distinct from others is the fact that she uses only the rarest primary gems and exquisite organics in precious metal. There are about 3,500 different minerals but only about 50 are used as gemstones. Generally, 12 gems are considered as key gems: ruby, emerald, sapphire, diamond, aquamarine, chrysoberyl, tourmaline, peridot, topaz, garnet, opal and pearl. Out of these, ruby, emerald, sapphire, diamond and natural pearl are considered primary gems and are the rarest.

Her signature jewels use these five rarest of gems, turquoise and some classic organics such as coral and amber. She says that these rarest of gems create magic as the spectral colours of white light, which do not get absorbed, are reflected back giving each a unique colour.

Very little jewellery made before the 18th century has survived and the best ancient jewels have their origins in Egypt, Rome, China and India. There is however, a striking similarity in all ancient and heritage jewellery in the use of gems. Almost all heritage jewellery is embedded with the five rarest gems in different shapes, sizes, cuts and settings. These five rare gems are fast disappearing and extremely expensive – the rarest coloured gems are in fact prized many times higher than the best colour/cut diamond.

Bhargava is also keenly interested in Indian art and crafts, especially traditional art forms. She is a collector of objet d'art ranging from paintings on tussar silk and patta paintings to crafted old silver plates from Varanasi and old silver figures. One can decipher her commitment to perpetuate India's heritage in her collection of rare art works.

At the Galleria VSB, an exclusive art gallery at Square One Mall, Saket, one can marvel at exclusive artworks and paintings by renowned artists from Orissa, Andhra Pradesh, Tamil Nadu and Delhi. The focus of her collection, which she has phrased as a "Heritage Collection" are the rarest works of art from Orissa and Varanasi.

She states that her collection of paintings and sculptures from Orissa were largely influenced by her association with the state since her husband happens to be a senior civil servant of the Orissa cadre. She feels Orissa has managed to continue their old-age traditions and has perhaps the most creative artists and craftsmen, who owing to their simplicity, have not received recognition they deserve.

Galleria VSB collection of artworks include paintings by Kailash Chandra Mehera, Gajendra Prasad Sahu, Kashinath Jena, Manas Jena, Kiran Mohindra, Raghunath Sahu, Surath Choudhury, Gauranga Bariki, Pradeep Patra, Nityanand Sahu and sculptures by Raghunath Mohapatra.

Kailash Chandra Mehera is the recipient of the National Award and the UNESCO Award and has exhibited in many countries. Gajendra Prasad Sahu has won many national and state awards and has designed and sculpted national sports awards including the Arjuna Award, Dhyanchand Award, Dronacharya Award and Tenzing Norgay Award. Kashinath Jena is well-known for his Gita Govinda-themed paintings

Sculptor Raghunath Mohapatra has been conferred with some of the highest national honours: the Padmashree and the Padma Bhushan.

The collection at Galleria VSB reflects depth, colour and texturing and most importantly positive energy. Every art work is titled and conveys a subtle message. Each sculpture is a treasure worth passing from generation to the next.

House of VSB also boasts of Café VSB, which is an European-style café providing the best coffee and freshly-prepared food.

A visit to the House of VSB is a unique experience, worth remembering for a long time. If you can afford signature jewels or a classic painting or a rare sculpture from the House of VSB, you can be assured that it will be treasured for many generations.

Boutiques in Shahpur Jat

and will pack fragile goods for safe transportation. Apart from the state emporia, the area also has individual shops often run by artisans' cooperatives and non-government organisations that sell a variety of eco-friendly handmade products.

Heritage bazars

Some of the lanes of Chandni Chowk still specialise in the luxury commodities they sold to Mughal-era nobility. Dariba (p78) is a lane of shops selling silver and gold jewellery. Khari Baoli (p79) is the road that holds Asia's largest spice market, and Kinari Bazaar sells sarees in every colour and material imaginable. These streets are a decidedly more vibrant – and more challenging – shopping experience than anywhere else in Delhi. Wear your game face. Haggling is expected, and the easiest bargaining tactic is

to quote half the asked price. In the southern part of town, Dilli Haat (pg 134) is a festive open market specialising in handicrafts; it's a great way to interact with actual artisans from across the country and pick up original handicrafts at low prices.

Mall strips

Delhi's first mall, Ansal Plaza on Khel Gaon Marg, kicked off mall culture in the city ten years ago. Today it feels like it's already been a century. They're the preferred retailing areas for international brands and leading Indian brands, and they provide invaluable respite from the heat, the human crush and the lack of public amenities in Delhi – its just unfortunate how unimaginative they are in design. They all look exactly like any mall off the New Jersey Turnpike. Yet the city's shopping malls, already the places

⌄HIDESIGN

Dilli Haat

where many wealthy and middle-class Dilliwalas automatically go to shop, are now becoming something much bigger: centres for cultural and social life. They are places you can go to see art and theatre as well as movies, for dancing lessons as well as drinking sessions, and to do yoga as well as to play pool.

Delhi has mall strips in four districts: Saket and Vasant Kunj in South West Delhi, Rajouri Gardens in West Delhi, and the satellite commerce-towns of Gurgaon and Noida. The most relevant are Select CityWalk in Saket (p147) and the DLF mall duo of Promenade and uber-luxe Emporio. Or just take the Metro to Gurgaon, where there's nothing else but malls.

Refunds

Always inquire before you buy. Most stores do not have refund or exchange policies.

Shipping

To send goods home, contact a cargo or shipping agency like UPS (2638-9323) or DHL (1800-111-345).

Delhi's original club
sensation, Elevate

WHAT'S BEST
Nightlife

Clubbing

Delhi's nightlife is thriving,
with local and international DJs
spinning at big dance venues
every weekend. The scene is still
largely dominated by the capitals'
many bars and lounges, rather
than proper nightclubs, even for
DJ nights. These include Delhi's
first true-blue lounge Shalom
(p174) and the social boiling pot
of 2010, Red Monkey (p154). But
don't overlook Delhi's creaky,
atmospheric old gin-joints like
Saqi (p120) or Golden Dragon
(p150) when you're looking for a
more affordable drink.

There are few real clubs, and
most of those are secluded in
five-star hotels. Stand-alone
restaurants, bars and clubs
within Delhi proper must close at
midnight, so you'll notice a lot of
late-night after partying at hotel
bars. On weekends, there's also a
nighttime exodus to the suburb-
cities of Noida and Gurgaon
(which are in different states,
and different excise jurisdictions).
Some hotels have been granted
24-hour liquor licenses as well,
letting you party till noon the
next day if you want.

Elevate was the first real club in
the National Capital Region; it's
now been replaced by the even
more steroidal Quantum (p204),
whose line-up is always worth

checking out. Currently, the very spiffy Lap (p118) in the Hotel Ashok keeps feet on the dancefloor until the sun is up and the birds are singing.

Spin city, live nation

The good news for fans of live music is that Delhi's once-barren gig calendar is now crammed with bands and live DJ and electronica acts. For guitar bands and straight-up rock music, head to venues like Turquoise Cottage (p154) for new talent, its upstart cousin Café Morrison (p150) for

drum 'n' bass and reggae acts and @live (p121) or Q'BA (p106) for soul, jazz and lounge acts.

Indian Ocean, Advaita and Menwhopause are some of Delhi's best-loved bands, and for a taster of capital rock, it's worth seeking them out. Rock and metal remain the mainstay of live music in the city, but increasingly, Delhi is making a name for itself as a cradle for new electronic music talent. Beloved local DJ acts like Jalebee Cartel, Midival Punditz and B.L.O.T. frequently play sold-out gigs in Berlin's biggest clubs,

@live

SHORTLIST

For a taste of Maui
Jolly Rogers (p194)

Unusual cocktails
Keya (p150)

Sushi while you drink
The Yum Yum Tree (p172)

New Delhi hipsters
The Living Room Café (p157)

Mellow Mediterranean-tinged lounging
Shalom (p174)

A house-party vibe
Red Monkey (p154)

An elegant evening
Olive (p152)

Fresh well-crafted cocktails
Smoke House Grill (p175)

Outdoor gig-nights
ai (p149)

Cool kids in a courtyard
The Zoo (p154)

Headbanging and live bands
Turquoise Cottage (p154)

Big-name DJs in a big club
Quantum (p204)

Drinks round the clock
24/7 at The Lalit hotel (p117)

Cocktails with the swish set
Lap (p118)

but can regularly be found playing for their home crowd. Quantum (p204), Shalom (p174) and ai (p149) have consistently crowded gig nights featuring big names, and a quick scout around any Delhi club will reveal that there's a fresh new batch of DJ talent waiting in the wings. Of this new crop, Kohra, Dualist Inquiry and Delhi Sultanate are acts worth catching. Even if you can't tell dubstep from techno, they'll keep you dancing into the wee hours and always make for big, fun, messy nights out.

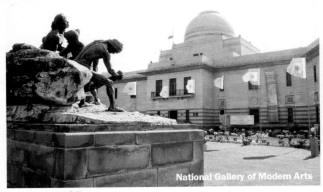

National Gallery of Modern Arts

WHAT'S BEST

Arts & Leisure

There's a popular joke that never grows old in Delhi: that the only culture we have is agriculture. It's a reference to how history turned the city from the capital of genteel and courtly Islamic culture into a modern city populated mainly by agrarian Punjabi refugees.

In reality, Delhi is swiftly catching up on Mumbai as the most culturally vibrant city in South Asia. The combination of ancient performance traditions, national government institutions and small creative enterprises is pushing the lid off this once-tepid melting pot. The best way to keep up with it, and learn what to see while you're in town, is with the fortnight's issue of *Time Out Delhi*, available at all magazine stands.

Art

The fine arts in Delhi generally refers to modern and contemporary art; outside of museums, there is little active interest in classical art and sculpture. But with a burgeoning number of galleries and artists, Delhi's contemporary art scene is thriving. While the National Gallery of Modern Art (p123) has a permanent display of Amrita Sher-Gil's works (one of Delhi's most expensive streets has also been named after this Indian Frida Kahlo), a host of private art galleries such as Vadehra Art Gallery (p175) ensure a wide variety of talent is brought out of the woodwork.

A lot of critical interest is directed at experimental galleries

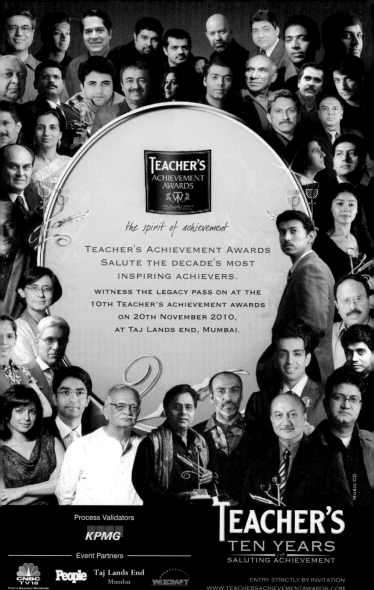

Arts & leisure

like Nature Morte (p156), the W+K gallery and the Devi Art Foundation (p195). The KHOJ Residency Workshop is at the forefront of new artistic directions, especially performance art, public art and new media. Smaller galleries in Delhi's emerging art districts – Lado Sarai (p157), also Shahpur Jat and Hauz Khas Village – swing the balance towards more affordable work.

Film

A number of large film festivals are held through the year in Delhi. In recent years, the major cinematic event has been Cinefan, produced by the Osian's art firm. It features cinema from India and around South East Asia. For current information on film festivals and screenings in the city, pick up *Time Out Delhi*.

Cinemas

Dilliwalas navigate many parts of the city by the names of old single-screen cinemas – Eros, Savitri, Upahaar – but few of these cinemas exist anymore. Most of the ones that do show B-grade Hindi films for working class audiences. But the antique Delite Cinema (p120) should still

Delite Cinema Hall

From the series *Noida Soliloquy*.
Courtesy: Dhruv Malhotra/PHOTOINK

be a delight to visit.

The rest of Delhi has moved on, with little sign of remorse, to the flashier multiplexes dotted around the city. The first modern multiplex in Delhi was the PVR Anupam, which went on to revolutionize India's movie screening industry. There are now over 20 multiplexes around town, with more being built, usually inside malls. Most newspapers carry cinema listings.

Music

Delhi's most vital, surviving link to its cultured Islamic past is qawwali, the Sufi devotional music still performed at dargahs (most famously Nizamuddin – p166 – but also many smaller shrines). The Jahan-e-Khusrau Sufi music festival is held every March, at the picturesque tomb of Humayun. But needless to say, Delhi's status as the national capital means that classical musicians of all kinds perform here. There are also large festivals devoted to jazz (the Jazz Utsav every December) and regional rock.

Theatre

Centred mostly around Mandi House (p123,125) near Connaught Place, Delhi's theatre scene benefits greatly from this being the capital city – national cultural institutions, embassies and the National School of Drama (NSD) are responsible for bringing some spectacular world theatre to Delhi stages. Theatre season, as with all of Delhi's performing arts, is November to February. The annual highlight is the NSD's Bharat Rang Mahotsav (www.nsdtheatrefest.com) , which runs through mid-January. Recently, the NSD festival has had to squeeze itself in between an annual festival dedicated to Ibsen (www.delhibsenfestival.com) and a wonderful festival of puppetry (www.isharapuppet.com).

Arts & leisure

Local theatre is undernourished, and tends to rely on serial repetitions of Neil Simon scripts or overperformed Hindi farce. Visitors with any Hindi or Urdu should look for performances of dastangoi, the traditional Persian-court storytelling, which has been brilliantly revived in recent years.

Outdoors

When the weather is good – and yes, it sometimes is, even here – there is no Indian city that rewards being outdoors like Delhi. Delhi is actually one of the greenest of India's metropolises, and one of the greenest capital cities in the world. It has an enviable tree cover, documented species-by-species in Pradeep Kishen's lushly produced volume *The Trees of Delhi*.

Its parks and gardens are wonderful places to spend time and watch Delhi's colourful civic life, especially central Delhi's Lodhi Gardens (p92) and Nehru Park, which frequently host music concerts. The outlying Garden of Five Senses (p131), has dedicated areas to showcase sculpture and live music, all under an open sky. Finally, Delhi's large forested area, the Ridge, attracts excursions of birdwatching enthusiasts. Contact the Delhi Bird Group at (98100-08625) or devasar@gmail.com.

Spas

The Mughal hammam was the original Delhi spa, but modern spas – most, but not all, located in hotels – have drawn more heavily on traditions from Kerala, Bali and Sweden. If you want your indulgence brought to you, ring up the Tattva mobile spa. An

SHORTLIST

Mystic's music
Nizamuddin dargah (p166)
Inayat Khan dargah (p165)

For the modern art canon
National Gallery of Modern Art (p123)

Art on the cutting edge
Nature Morte (p156)
Devi Art Foundation (p195)

For snapping up some photography
PhotoInk (p183)

Best old-school cinema
Delite (p120)

Best for theatre and dance
Kamani Theatre (p123)
Stein Auditorium,
India Habitat Centre (p122)

For pressing appointments
Amatrra spa (p122)

Ayurvedic attentions
Kairali spa (p155)

over-the-phone consultation allows the Tattva crew to decide what's best for you (treatments begin from ₹2000), and on the appointed day and time, two therapists, complete with massage tables, scented candles, music and rose petals breeze in and convert your room into a sanctuary. *Call Tattva at (6499-4126, 99998-35852) or visit www.tattvaspa.com.*

Itineraries

Gali Matia Mahal

The Mughal trail: The Walled City

Shah Jahan's city is a retail heaven, an ethnographer's delight and a sensory overload. Its central thoroughfare, Chandni Chowk, branches off into a warren of different neighbourhoods, traditionally divided by religious community, profession or trade. Specialised markets, wholesale shops and old havelis (mansions) are punctuated by historic monuments and places to eat. Vendors specialising in street food indigenous to Shahjahanabad enjoy local and even international fame. This walk combines a few historic gems with some culinary delights, which, unfortunately, are not for the weak-stomached (though they can all be visually appreciated). If you get lost, ask someone, or hail a cycle-rickshaw (₹10-50 per stretch). You can also pick and choose locales from this itinerary to explore, as the whole walk is ambitious for one day.

From Rajiv Chowk Metro station at Connaught Place, take the yellow line to Chandni Chowk station and follow the crowd out to the main avenue, **Chandni Chowk**. If you're touring the Red Fort (p71) in the morning, you can start from the east end of Chandni Chowk, just opposite the fort. Ask for the **Old Famous Jalebiwala**, a century-old counter that sells jalebis (orange fried sweets). The stall is on the corner of Chandni Chowk and **Dariba Kalan** (p78) – a jewellers' area. The surrounding area, called Dharampura, is home to the Old City's Jain population and is dotted with Jain temples. The most famous, the early 18th-century Lal Mandir, at the eastern end of Chandni Chowk, opposite

the Red Fort), is just as well known for its **bird hospital** (p70) as for the temple itself. Browse antique silver jewellery as you walk down Dariba Kalan – keep asking for the right turn to the Kinari Bazaar. Walk down that colourful haberdashers' street, festooned with tinsel, embellishments for clothing, beads and ribbons, keeping an eye on an opening into a cul-de-sac on your left. **Naughara** (p72) is a little enclave of jewellers' havelis, some remarkably well maintained. The enclave gives you an idea of how the area may have looked decades ago. At the end of the street, on the right, is the Jauhri Temple, a Jain "jeweller's temple".

Take a look inside the two-level building, which was built in the late 18th century and renovated later. The paintings seem to be influenced by a synthesis of various traditions, including Mughal miniature painting. Exit

Naughara

The Sky Waltz Experience

A recent ad said, "When was the last time you did something for the first time?" Well, I just did. I took my maiden flight in a hot air balloon with Sky Waltz. And I don't think I've really come down to earth yet!

Our Sky Waltz Experience began pretty early that morning, when their cheerful crew came and picked us up at our hotel. My friends and I were brimming with anticipation and threw a barrage of questions at the crew, which they answered happily.

Soon, we reached the launch site and were greeted with a scene of bustling activity. The mammoth balloons were being unwrapped and we immediately whipped out our cameras to record this unusual sight. We met our pilot, who gave us a short safety briefing and outlined some of the mechanics of what we were about to see and experience. He then got busy lighting the burners and the fire began to heat up the air inside the balloon. The fabric swelled out majestically, the balloon became upright and our air chariot was ready for us.

We were helped into the basket by the polite ground crew and made ourselves comfortable. Then, it seemed as if someone released the invisible ropes that tied us down, we swayed a little, there was a sudden flare of flames above us… and we were up, up and away.

We were lifted gently, watching the earth fall away below us. Soon, we were flying over forts and castles, craggy mountains, sandy stretches and green plains. We dipped down to kiss the waters of a limpid lake, then floated up again. We flew over towns and villages, even spotted a herd of deer. None of us had ever seen the world from this perspective. There's no rush, no urgency, no whirring of engines. It's peaceful, serene and incredibly beautiful.

There's no feeling quite like it, nothing on earth that can match the magic of floating on air, the sense of being at one with the sky and looking down at a world that is looking up at you!

Before we knew it, our hour-long flight was over and the pilot found us a nice landing site on the outskirts of a local village - "We very rarely land in the same place twice, it's always a different group of friendly locals with wide-eyed amazement" the pilot proudly announced. The retrieval crew was on hand to receive us and we each got a Certificate of First Flight duly signed by the pilot.

Sky Waltz is the first Government Authorised commercial Hot Air Balloon Company in India. The pilot told us that Sky Waltz has sourced their balloons from overseas. Their pilots are from Europe, UK, Australia and the USA, with thousands of hours of balloon piloting behind them. Besides being really friendly, the ground crew has been trained and equipped to match the standards of the best crews internationally.

Their safety norms are identical to those followed anywhere in the world. The entire project has been set up under the advisory services of well-known consultants from overseas. We had booked our flight through our hotel, but you can also book flights on their website or through travel agents.

Sky Waltz gave us an exhilarating, soaring, unforgettable experience.

Fatehpuri Masjid

the cul-de-sac and continue down Kinari Bazaar until you reach **Paranthewali Gali** (p75) on your right. Keep an eye out for a man with a big basket of white and yellow milk foam. This delicate confection, known as daulat ki chaat, is built up of layers of whipped milk foam, sprinkled with brown sugar and pistachios topped with edible silver leaf. The street is named for the several parantha specialists here. If you do want to eat, stop at the cramped eatery of **Pandit Babu Ram Devi Dayal** (p75). Eventually, you'll emerge on to Chandni Chowk. Cross the street and turn right, and you'll come to **Ghantewala Sweets** (p75) on your right. This shop, established in 1790 and said to have catered to Mughal emperors, sells delicious sohan halwa – sweet roundels of brown sugar and ghee. A little further ahead, at the fountain, is **Gurdwara Sis Ganj** (p70), an important Sikh temple, built on the site of the martyrdom of one of the Sikh spiritual leaders, Guru Tegh Bahadur.

Double back on Chandni Chowk or take a green minibus to the western end of the street at Fatehpuri (keep an eye out for the Town Hall, built in 1866, on your right). In front of you, at the intersection, is **Fatehpuri Masjid**, built in 1650 by Fatehpuri Begum, one of Shah Jahan's wives. The large mosque and madrasa complex is worth a visit. If you're facing the complex, take a right and then a left on to **Khari Baoli** (p79), the wholesale spice market. Straight past the left turn is **Giani's** – famous since 1951 for the kulfi falooda (traditional ice-cream topped with sweet vermicelli).

From Fatehpuri, walk down Khari Baoli, past sneeze-inducing piles of ground and whole chillis, turmeric, peppers and murabbas (fruit preserves). From here, take a rickshaw and ask for **Hamdard**

Inherited Legacy...
Experienced Royally!!

SkyWaltz Balloon Safari

JAIPUR • RANTHAMBHORE • PUSHKAR • NEEMRANA • NCR OF DELHI

www.skywaltz.com

For information and bookings please contact :
Toll Free (8am to 8pm) 1800 102 2366
goballooning@skywaltz.com

FACTOR
E-Factor Adventure Tourism (P) Limited

FRASER SUITES
— N E W   D E L H I —

Frasers aims to be the premier global leader in the extended stay market through our commitment to continuous innovation in answering the unique needs of every customer.

Experience the difference with special residence features of Fraser Suites, New Delhi

- 92 Fully furnished serviced residences with integrated living, dining and kitchen
- Wireless Internet Access
- Exclusive elevator access to residences with security keycard system
- In-room safe
- iPod docking with alarm clock
- Comprehensive home entertainment system:
  - LED TV
  - Satellite, cable network - local and international TV channels
  - DVD player
  - Audio system
- Well-equipped kitchen:
  - Electric hob and hood
  - Refrigerator/Freezer
  - Microwave/oven
  - Washer/dryer

- Business complements:
  - Fully equipped business center with meeting facilities
  - The Retreat – An award winning business facility infusing business with pleasure
- Lifestyle amenities:
  - Health club with pool deck
  - Swimming pool
  - Fitness center
  - Café - The Dining Room

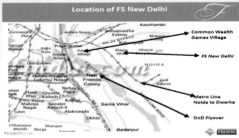

Location of FS New Delhi

frasershospitality.com

FRASER SUITES
─ NEW DELHI ─

THE NEW HOME OF AWARD-WINNING FRASERS HOSPITALITY.

Redefine your lifestyle at New Delhi's first international
extended-stay serviced apartment, located at Mayur Vihar

RESERVATIONS: 1800 103 9977

frasershospitality.com

Ghantewala Sweets

Dawakhana. You'll go down **Naya Bans Street**, passing the paan (betel leaf) wholesale market. Continue via rickshaw, keeping an eye out for the first-floor **Masjid Mubarak Begum**, built in 1823 by one of the wives of Sir David Ochterlony, the first British Resident of Delhi, down to **Hauz Qazi Chowk**, the intersection where the Chawri Bazaar Metro station is located. Walk a little bit down **Bazaar Sita Ram** and turn right at Kucha Pati Ram, a narrow, quiet street that leads to **Lala Dulli Chand Naresh Gupta** (p76), who sells fruit kulfis in flavours from pomegranate to mango. Back out on Bazaar Sita Ram, take a longish rickshaw ride down to the **Kalan Masjid**, which was one of seven identical mosques built in 1387 by Khan-i-Jehan Jujan Shah, prime minister to the Tughlak ruler Feroze Shah. The mosque is painted in bright blue, purple, turquoise and green, has a marble courtyard fountain

with goldfish swimming in the green water and a marvellous view from the roof (ask the imam if you can climb up).

From here, it's another long but interesting rickshaw ride via a wholesale paper market to **Jama Masjid** (p70). India's largest mosque, built in 1656 by Shah Jahan. Nearby is **Bazaar Matia Mahal**, which houses the famous **Karim Hotel** (see p74), which claims to have been founded by imperial Mughal cooks. Try the mutton burra kebabs or a korma with sheermal, a sweetish bread. Opposite Karim's you'll see a few stalls selling shahi tukda, Delhi's most unholy bread pudding, loaded with sugar, heavy cream and a pool of ghee. Take a rickshaw to the Chawri Bazaar Metro station to bring you back to Connaught Place.

For a guided walk of Chandni Chowk contact INTACH at 011-2463-2267 or visit www.intachdelhichapter.org.

The Sultanate trail: Mehrauli

The area around Mehrauli isn't just home to designer boutiques. If you're the historical sort but have time for only one big walk, we'd recommend a stroll around **Mehrauli**. It gives you a sweeping look back at Delhi's history, with monuments dating from the Sultanate period in the thirteenth century right down to those built by the British in the mid-nineteenth century. Old structures and ruins are scattered like breadcrumbs here and there is little chance that anyone will manage seeing all of it in one day. We suggest you walk around the monuments within and around the Mehrauli Archaeological Park.

Cross the road at **Ahimsa Sthal** on the Mehrauli-Gurgaon Road. This is easy to locate as the massive granite statue of Mahavir (founder of the Jain faith) is visible from the road

itself. On the other side, walk southwards till you come to the park gate with its signboard listing various prohibited activities (plucking flowers and cooking, among others). Once inside, you'll find a gateway leading to Balban's tomb on your right. **Balban** was one of the Slave sultans and his tomb (dating back to 1286AD) is significant because this crumbling structure apparently features the first true arch in India. The tomb has three chambers and the central room was supposed to have housed Balban's grave, which is now missing. The smaller chamber to its east is said to have been the burial place for his son, Khan Shahid. There is a cenotaph in the western wing of the building. Nearby you can see excavations of a residential settlement. Walking westwards, you come across two tombs. One of these is believed to be the actual resting place of Khan Shahid.

Jamali Kamali

The ruins of Balban's Tomb

Turn right from here and walk on to the **Jamali Kamali** mosque and tomb (p133), possibly the best maintained and most beautiful of all the structures inside the park. Jamali was the pen-name of Shaikh Hamid bin Fazluddin, a poet from the Lodhi and early Mughal periods. He himself built the structures in 1528-'29 and was buried here when he died in 1536. Besides Jamali's grave, the tomb also contains Kamali's grave. No one knows who this person is, though some believe that Kamali was Jamali's gay lover. The tomb is locked, and you need permission from the Archaeological Survey of India to enter.

From outside the Jamali Kamali complex, you can see a canopy atop a mound to the east. This hexagonal structure was built by Sir Thomas Metcalfe, British Resident at Delhi's court during the 1840s, and is an excellent vantage point from which to survey the surrounding

monuments. Inspired by English country manors that had "follies", Metcalfe built some himself, despite the fact that there were so many genuinely old monuments here anyway.

Retrace your steps to Khan Shahid's tomb and walk northwards. Along the way you'll find various tombs, mosques, wall mosques and other structures, most of which are in a dilapidated state. The road will turn eastwards until you arrive at **Rajon Ki Baoli** (p133). This step-well was supposedly used by masons (raj) at one time, hence the name. It's a beautiful oblong structure, with steps leading down to the water, and is surrounded by lush greenery. Only three of its four storeys are now visible. Linked to the baoli are a mosque and a pillared-tomb.

Walk down the path, with the baoli on your right until you see small stone columns pointing the way towards **Metcalfe's Bridge**.

The Tibetan Market at Janpath

Further on is a small ruined house on the right. This is said to be from the Lodhi era and was modified by Metcalfe into a boathouse and dovecote. On the left are steep steps leading up to **Quli Khan's tomb**, who was apparently the emperor Akbar's foster brother. Metcalfe bought this octagonal structure, named it Dilkhusha and converted it into his country retreat. He made additions to the structure, some of which are still standing. Around **Dilkhusha** are ruined buildings, which he used as guest quarters.

If you walk down the steps towards the north, the **Chaumu-kha Darwaza** will appear on your right. This gateway has arched openings on all four sides and is probably from the Tughlaq period. You can cross the narrow drain nearby and walk further till you come to a modern iron gate.

We left the park here and turned right towards the main road. Readers in better shape than us could buy a ticket and step into the **Qutab Minar** (p132) complex. There's another couple of hours' worth of exploration right there.

The souvenir hunt: Connaught Place

Begin this trail right outside the **Imperial Hotel** (p209). Turn your back on its manicured grounds and stroll up ahead to where the **Tibetan Market** begins. Apart from various Tibetan souvenirs – allegedly antique thangkhas (painted Buddhist scrolls), brass Buddha statues, prayer beads and bells – there are tons of other knick-knacks to pick up. Look out for pretty anklets with tiny bells on the pavement, and printing blocks with beautiful carvings of animals on them. Even if you're not in the mood to shop, this stretch of road makes for an easy, jostle-free walk.

After the Tibetan market, cross **Tolstoy Marg**, and you come to a gloriously touristy souvenir shop selling everything from mini Taj Mahals to sandalwood incense. We particularly like the colourful cloth lamps. They're perfect to brighten up a corner at home and come in all shapes and sizes with appliqué and cut-work designs. This is where **Janpath Market** (p113) starts, with its shoe shops. Try the multicoloured handmade leather slippers called Kohlapuris, pretty scarves, psychedelic tees with various calendar art on them.

Soon, you'll come to more open ground, where the **Janpath Bhavan** market complex is located. Local students populate their wardrobe from the line of clothes stalls selling export rejects that have the latest trends. The row of shops continues after this, and includes a handmade paper shop (the lightweight paper

products are great present to take back home for friends), a perfume and incense store and **Tantra** (also at p109), which sells some witty, and sometimes cheesy, "India"-inspired T-shirts.

At Connaught Place (Outer Circle), take a left toward the **Jeevan Bharati** building. This nice, leafy stretch is perfect for a stroll. Have your palm read by the fortune-teller in the subway while crossing to the **Regal** block. We suggest you take a quick detour here to the left, past the Barista café, to **People Tree** (p112), where you can stock up on eco-friendly casual wear, bags, accessories, hats and hair bands. The focus here is on selling natural fabrics and dyes and the tees usually have social and environmental messages on them. Backtrack towards Regal Cinema once you're done browsing here. There are weight-telling machines at the entrance of the cinema hall.

People Tree

Itineraries

One rupee slipped into the slot will give you your weight and your fortune. While the former isn't important, the fortunes are fun to read.

While the rest of the Outer Circle does make for an engaging wander, if you aren't in the mood, take a rickshaw (or the metro) to **Paharganj Main Bazaar** (p115), near the New Delhi Railway Station. Located directly opposite the station, Paharganj is the best stop for the cheapest backpacker and hippie chic. Walk down the Paharganj Main Bazaar. There are rows of shops on both sides selling everything from bags, shoes and clothes, to psychedelic accessories. If you're interested in belly dancing, stop by at

Shri Krishna Arts, which has everything from costumes to classes.

If all that walking has tired you out, stop at **Sam's Café** for a quick bite. Try the apple crumble if you're in the mood for some serious sugar. A little further down is **All Indian Handicrafts** on your right, selling "tribal" handicrafts from across the country. Of the many second-hand bookstores here, our favourite is **Jacksons Books** (p115), which stocks volumes in at least 30 languages.

The Paharganj market is just a single, winding, very crowded stretch, but if you're a Goa-bound hippie at heart, no other trail will warm your heart like this one.

Pipes on sales
in Paharganj

Delhi by Area

North Delhi

Coronation Park

Majnu ka Tilla

THE MARK OF THE EMPIRE

North Delhi was an area of villages, orchards and aristocratic estates that spread out before the northernmost gate of Shah-jahanabad (called Kashmere Gate, because of its orientation toward Kashmir). It became the first bastion of the British in Delhi, and their heritage has seeped longest into this soil.

This is where it was first proposed that New Delhi be built in 1911, and long before that the British either lived in or ruled over Delhi from the Civil Lines area. After the mutiny of 1857, their bloody reconquest of Delhi came down through Kashmere Gate. Even today it is the University district – one of the more benign British legacies – and home of Delhi's oldest colleges.

The Coronation Park, the memorial to the Empire and its administrators, lies in a sort of moral exile at Delhi's northernmost point. Today North Delhi is an area of violent contrasts: serene colonial-era graveyards tucked around a heaving Inter-state Bus Terminal and transport centre; the tree-lined avenues of Civil Lines and the howling Grand Trunk Road highway; the St Stephens College and the Tibetan refugee village, Majnu Ka Tilla. It's always been a favourite for doughtier adventurers, but it's much easier to visit now that the Metro runs right up through it.

Sights & Museums

Coronation Park This field was the site of numerous imperial darbars, culminating in the Coronation Darbar of 1911, where the new King James V personally introduced himself and announced the construction of an imperial capital in Delhi. Today it's a powerfully desolate expanse, with one corner filled with statuary of the King and eminent administrators, moved here from other parts of the city. The great obelisk of the Coronation Memorial stands where James once stood, addressing nothing but grass and puddles. A moving sight if you're excited by history, but not easy to get to. ⊖ *GTB Nagar, then ask an auto to take you toward the Outer Ring Road. Look out for the obelisk; the gate is unmarked. Sunrise-sundown.* ❶

STADIUM Delhi University Sports Complex Rugby 7s. ⊖ *Vishwavidyalaya* ❷.

Nicholson Cemetery Only metres from the Kashmere Gate Bus Terminal lies one of the earliest British cemeteries in India, the Nicholson Cemetery, named after Brigadier General John Nicholson who led the recapture of Delhi in 1857. The cemetery is in a state of some neglect, but its many memorials and tombstones are still impressive. Nicholson's grave is just near the entrance on the right when you enter the cemetery's gates. Be careful of the stray monkeys around the place, although they aren't aggressive unless teased. It's right beside the Kashmere Gate Metro station. *Lala Hardev Sahai Marg.* ⊖ *Kashmere Gate* ❸

Nicholson Cemetery

St James Church Colonel James Skinner was the foremost military personality of nineteenth-century Delhi. Born and raised in India, he was rejected by the East India Company because of his mixed blood, and fought for the Maratha kings instead. He raised a regiment called Skinner's Horse, which still exists in the Indian Army today as the 1st Bengal Cavalry.

According to legend, he once took a battlefield vow to build a magnificent church, and the outcome is St James Church near Kashmere Gate. Built between 1826-1836, the building is a blend of European architecture with Indian motifs: look out for Mughal-inspired floral motifs in marble and the the military insignia of the regiment on the lectern. The front pews are still reserved for Skinner's descendants. There is no admission fee, but the caretaker who opens the Church appreciates a tip.

St James Church, Kashmere Gate, crossing of Church Road and Lothian Road (2332-0005).
⊖ Kashmere Gate ❹

St James Church

DELHI BY AREA

Ladakh Buddha Vihara

Ladakh Buddha Vihara This monastery, inaugurated by India's first prime minister Jawaharlal Nehru in 1963, is a monument to Delhi's status as refuge for Tibetan exiles. The building was constructed with the participation of Kushok Gyalras Bakula, a member of Tibetan royalty. Since its renovation in 1990, the monastery has been an oasis of calm beside the bustling Tibetan market nearby. There is a massive prayer wheel by the main gate, living quarters for monks and a garden in front of the vihara. The vihara is generally devoid of visitors except during Buddha Purnima and Buddha Jayanti. *Bela Road.* ♙ *Civil Lines* ❺

ફરિયાદ / સૂચના
અહીં નોંધશો

Shree Delhi Gujarati Samaj canteen

Eating & Drinking

Embassy The new Embassy Restaurant is a slightly jazzed up but still old-world version of the Connaught Place branch. Serving only Indian food unlike its multi-cuisine elder sibling, the restaurant has been done up in colonial club style. Inside, the décor is minimal and classic; the walls are cool and dark, set on one side with rough but shiny grotto-esque stones. The murg pakeeza from the appetiser menu (₹230) is easily the best thing to order, and the gravy of the malai kofta (₹200) is a deliciously smooth concoction of cashews, onions and yogurt with a honeyed aftertaste. There's probably a bit of a learning curve until the establishment catches up to the elegantly matter-of-fact CP branch. But it's definitely a good place for a starving visitor to stop by for a cold Kingfisher (₹200). *13 Alipur Road, Civil Lines (2399-3061).* ⊖ *Civil Lines. Open for lunch noon-3.30pm; dinner 7.30pm-12.30am. Alcohol not served. Meal for two ₹1,200. All major credit cards accepted.* ⊙

Shree Delhi Gujarati Samaj canteen The unlimited thali here (₹35) is reputed to be the most authentic Gujarati grub in the city. It's also one the few places you'll find the ghee-filled khichdi that Emperor Jehangir is said to have loved. The Mahila Samaj runs a counter here selling a range of excellent fresh pickles, masalas and chutneys like golkeri. *2 Rajniwas Marg, Civil Lines (2398-1796)* ⊖ *Civil Lines. Daily 10.30am-10.30pm. Thali ₹35.* ⊙

Majnu Ka Tilla

Shopping

Majnu ka Tilla The Tibetan shop-owners who dominate the Majnu ka Tilla market have lived in Delhi for decades, but in the endless rows of their stalls, the goods still speak of a Himalayan homeland, whether they are little brass rings (₹50), warm woollen jackets ostensibly made of 100 per cent Yak hair (₹150-450) or commercial trekking gear like hiking boots, tents and sleeping bags. There are several restaurants where you can get a bite to eat while you're on the move, but it might be safest to ask for TD's. Consider the chhurpi, yak-cheese cubes, stone-hard and tasting like nothing at all. They're held between the teeth to dissolve, providing nourishment and keeping up salivation when moving in mountainous terrian. Much softer than Yak-cheese are the shawls (₹500-750) and carpets (₹400), available at almost every corner. You can even find a leather horse saddle (₹4000) brought down from Tibet. Naturally, the Majnu ka Tilla market also offers shoppers ways to demonstrate their cultural or political solidarity to Tibet: prayer flags and prayer wheels, as well as posters and scarves stamped with the flag of independent Tibet. *Dr Hedgewar Marg. Daily 10am-10pm.* ⊖ *Vishwavidyalaya* ⑧

Arts & Leisure

Sarai CSDS Sarai, an initiative of the Centre for the Study of Developing Societies, is a leading watering hole for Delhi's young intelligentsia. Since it was set up in 2000, it has experimented with a variety of scholarly and creative practices, usually centred around cities and urban existence, and Delhi in particular. A small space in its charming Civil Lines building is reserved for the short-term exhibition of experimental media work, installation art and other often-audacious inquiries into software, radio, performance art, writing and music. These exhibitions are usually themed with a larger conference or event. The seminar and screening space also hosts a regular and curated schedule of screenings of video copies of films, followed by discussions.
29 Rajpur Road, Civil Lines (2392-8391). ⊖ *Civil Lines.* ⑨

Sarai CSDS

DELHI BY AREA

Old Delhi

Sunrise at Jama Masjid

Chattah Chowk

MODERN LIFE IN THE MUGHAL CITY

What everybody calls Old Delhi – or Purani Dilli, in Hindi – isn't the oldest Delhi by a long shot. From the seventeenth century until 100 years ago, the city of Shahjahanabad was Delhi itself, and all around were the ruins and relics of older Delhis. Named after the Mughal emperor Shah Jahan, who had it built as a new capital, this was a city of palaces and poets. Even today, Delhi's historical picture of itself is as Shahjahanabad in its heyday.

Since the end of Mughal rule in 1857, the splendidly planned city has steadily fallen apart, so much so that by 1962 the municipal authorities had it categorised as a slum. Although it's in truly lamentable condition, Old Delhi is tailor-made for sightseers. With glorious mosques, chaotic bazars, shocking poverty and a constantly changing aroma – spices, food, humanity – it's a sensory assault that doesn't know when to quit. The rich, meaty Mughal cuisine is available everywhere, as are more specialised dishes, like paranthas, which have a lane devoted solely to them. There are also streets devoted to traditional commodities like spices and gems. The marvel of Old Delhi is how much it shows its age, but still manages to be so attractive.

the taste of
bengal

COME ENJOY AUTHENTIC BENGALI
AND ANGLO-INDIAN CUISINE FROM
THE BHADRALOK KITCHEN

Brown Sahib

2nd Floor, MGF Metropolitan Mall, Saket, New Delhi
011-40820027, 011-40820028
walk through S.Oliver Showroom to enter from Select City Walk Mall)

Sights & Museums

Charity Birds Hospital Right across from the Red Fort is an unusual attraction: a hospital for birds and rabbits, founded by a Jain sect in 1956. Go all the way upstairs to see the "general ward", a feeding frenzy; there's even an intensive-care ward and a research laboratory (no carnivorous birds are admitted, though). Bathed, fed, and given vitamins, the healthy birds often refuse to leave, and that's how you can spot the building – by the flocks swirling around its roof. Keep in mind it's a real hospital, so its not exactly Bambi inside.
Digambar Jain Temple, Netaji Subhash Marg, opposite Red Fort (2328-0942). Daily 8am-8pm. Entry free. ⊖ *Chandni Chowk* ❶

Gurdwara Sis Ganj Sahib
One of the most important Sikh shrines in the world, this was where, on the main promenade of Chandni Chowk, the ninth Sikh spiritual leader Tegh Bahadur was executed in 1675. The gurdwara was built in 1861, then demolished, then rebuilt in 1930. Apart from the central prayer hall where the Granth Sahib (the holy book of the Sikh faith) is kept, the complex holds the well where guru Teg Bahadur took his last bath and the banyan tree under which he was said to have been beheaded.

Right next door to Sis Ganj is the Bhai Mati Das Sati Das Dyala Museum, where nearly a hundred oil paintings illustrate the history of the Sikh faith and explain its martial reputation.

Chandni Chowk (2326-6589).
⊖ *Chandni Chowk* ❷

Jama Masjid The largest mosque in India was built by Emperor Shah Jahan at a cost of about a million rupees (a lot of money in 1650). Constructed in sandstone and white marble, Jama Masjid is iconic of Delhi's Islamic life and heritage, and especially of the Eid celebration (during the month of Ramzan, the high walls are strung with lights and the solemn prayer courtyard becomes a giant picnic). Inside, its prayer hall is a marvel, its façade of 11 arches topped by three magnificent striped domes. Nearly 20,000 people can be accommodated in the masjid, and on Friday evenings it will feel like more. For a breath of air, ascend the southern minaret for a stunning view over the Old City.
⊖ *Chawri Bazar. Open sunrise-*

Jama Masjid

sunset, but entry restricted during prayers. Entry free. ❸

Kotla Firoz Shah This was the citadel of Firozabad, the fifth city of Delhi, built by Firoz Shah Tughlaq in the 1350s. Due to much later pillaging of stones (including to build Shahjahanabad nearby) the complex is largely in ruins. But there are still many wonders to see, including a virtually intact circular baoli (step well), a still-functioning mosque, and a pyramidal structure atop which stands one of the Buddhist emperor Ashoka's inscribed monolithic pillars, preserved by Firoz Shah. Firoz Shah Kotla is also the site of a religious practice unique to Delhi, where people deposit multiple photocopies of petitions addressed to jinns. *Bahadur Shah Zafar Marg, near Firoz Shah Kotla Stadium. Indian citizens and SAARC visitors ₹5, others ₹100. Children below 15 enter free.* ❹

The Red Fort Much of this immense fortress, the citadel of Shah Jahan, was destroyed in 1857. A more recent misfortune to befall the Red Fort has been its presentation as a monument of the Indian freedom struggle (this is where the national flag was first raised in 1947) rather than of the Mughal era. Built of red sandstone and embellished with intricate stone and marble work, this massive edifice dominates the eastern view of Old Delhi. With a good guide, it's an absorbing walk through the different royal quarters and halls where Shah Jahan held court. It was the

DELHI BY AREA

The walls of the Red Fort

DELHI BY AREA

political heart of the Mughal empire until 1857, when the British razed much of it and converted parts into barracks.

There are three museums within the complex: the Indian War Memorial Museum, with swords, muskets and other ancient armaments; the Mumtaz Mahal Museum of manuscripts and miniature paintings; and the Swatantrata Senani Museum, a memorial to the Indian National Army, which joined with the Axis powers to fight for independence. Much more cheerful is the hour-long sound-and-light show, which literally illuminates the spectacular history of the place. ↔ *Chandni Chowk. Tue-Sun 10am-5pm. Indian citizens ₹11, others ₹100. Sound-and-light show: Nov-Jan daily 7.30 pm, Jan-Apr 8.30pm, May-Aug 9pm, Sept & Oct 8.30pm. ₹11.* ❺

Naughara Stumbling on Naughara is like finding a diamond in the rough-and-tumble of Old Delhi. Literally. Amidst Chandni Chowk's congested capillaries, Naughara ("nine houses") is a stretch of brilliantly painted havelis, many of which now operate as jewellery boutiques. But the houses are the real gems here. Each is a different pastel shade, making the lane shine in contrast to the grubbiness outside.

The inside of one haveli, owned by Atam Agarwal, is festooned with antique furniture and ancient bric-a-brac. The house has more than a hundred doors and 50 windows, a portal into another era of Delhi.

***Atam Enterprises** 1998 Naughara, Kinari Bazar, near Parathewala Gali (2326-7052). Call ahead, timings vary.* ↔ *Chandni Chowk* ❻

Zeenat-ul-Masjid The Zeenat-ul-Masjid made a cameo appearance in one of the most memorable scenes in any Delhi film, where Leela Naidu hangs up her washing in *The Householder*. The masjid was built in 1707 by Zeenat-un-Nissa, the daughter of Mughal emperor Aurangzeb. After 1857, the British Army – concerned about the masjid as a dangerous congregational space – used it as a bakery, and even as stables and a tonga garage. Today the mini-replica of the Jama Masjid is used for Friday prayers but is empty the rest of the time. When asking locals for directions, remember to ask for the Ghata Masjid (cloud mosque). *Ansari Road, Daryaganj, opposite Shakti Sthal. Daily 10am-5pm. Entry free.* ❼

Eating & Drinking

Some of the earliest accounts of food in Delhi come from the fourteenth-century traveller Ibn Battuta's journals. Delhi court cuisine was an amalgam of Central Asian (Turkic, Persian etc) and local cooking techniques, creating what we know today as Mughlai food. But while Muslim cuisine is the best recorded, there's also an inventive vegetarian tradition, mostly belonging to the Banias, particularly Marwaris, and Khatris of Old Delhi. The hallowed tradition of Dilli chaat may have come from the Bania community. Newer traditions of Punjabi and frontier food, with the attendant popularity of chicken and tandoori items, have been added to the mix since Partition.

Mughlai & kababs

Babu Bhai Kababwale If you're sufficiently adventurous, meander down Matia Mahal Road to where it forks, and turn into Chitli Qabar. Mohammad Shakir peers out at you from a miniscule subterranean shop at Masjid Sayed Rafai, while roasting and

Zeenat-ul-Masjid

Street-side kababs in the Old City

Lala Dulli Chand
Naresh Gupta fruit kulfi

grilling his kababs. The spiced beef sutli kababs (₹5) are so meltingly tender, they're tied to the skewer with thread (sutli). Shakir also sells chewy "heart" tikkas, considerately providing squares of newsprint to wipe your fingers on.
1465-B, near Masjid Sayed Rafai, Bazaar Chilli Qabar (98993-2993). ✆ *Chawri Bazar.* ⓼

Al Jawahar Named after Jawaharlal Nehru, this is the first of a quartet of the area's now-legendary Mughlai restaurants. Some purists (or revisionists, depending on where you stand) vouch that it is better than the over-hyped Karim's next door – less rushed and, because Al-Jawahar was founded by a family of butchers, serving better cuts of meat. Mutton nihari and paya (trotters) are only served in the mornings. In the evenings, try the mutton burra, the robust shammi

kababs (₹25), or the gently-spiced and tender seekh kababs.
65 Bazar Matia Mahal, opposite Gate 1 Jama Masjid (2326-9241). ✆ *Chawri Bazar. Daily 7am-midnight. Meal for two ₹300.* ⓽

Karim's Hotel Karim's has a reputation that is truly awesome, but even so it never disappoints. The restaurant, home of the famous burra kababs and mutton qorma, has colonised every corner of Gali Kababian. Karim's outlets now exist all over the city, doing some damage to the novelty of the experience, but none of them compare to the clamour and excitement of eating at Karim's in the heart of Mughal Delhi.
16 Gali Kababian, Bazar Matia Mahal, opposite Gate 1 Jama Masjid (2326-9880). ✆ *Chawri Bazar. Daily 7am-midnight. Meal for two ₹300.* ⓵⓪

Vegetarian meals

Adarsh Bhojanalaya The few sit-down places to eat home-style food in the old city are Marwari-style restaurants. At Adarsh, order the separate special tadka

along with your unlimited thali.
*483 Haider Quli Corner, below
Andhra Bank, Chandni Chowk
(2398-7576).* ⊖ *Chandni Chowk.
Daily 10.30am-6pm; 6-11pm.* ⓫

Kake di Hatti This nondescript
but famous eatery was opened six
decades ago, serving a lunch thali
that's minimal but memorable:
the rotis simply enormous, the dal
makhani legendary, and Kake's 11
kinds of parantha, whole wheat
breads, stuffed with spicy fillings
and fried perfectly on a griddle.
*654 Church Mission Road,
Fatehpuri (98109-09754).*
⊖ *Chandni Chowk. Daily
7.30am-12.30pm.* ⓬

Paranthewali Gali A tiny
alleyway off Chandni Chowk
is lined with venerable eateries
dedicated to the art of the
parantha. The most famous is
Pandit Babu Ram Devi Dayal's,
where the mixed parantha and
the mattar (peas) parantha are
revelations about the fried bread.

**Tikka and
seekh kababs at
Karim's Hotel**

As an alternative, try **Nirmal
Restaurant**'s paneer parathas
(₹16), some of the best around.
Even better, there are three large
rooms to eat in with a view across
the Town Hall chowk.
*Nirmal Restaurant Paranthewali
Gali, 756 Chandni Chowk, opposite
Town Hall. Daily 6.30am-
midnight.* ⓭
*Pandit Babu Ram Devi Dayal
Paranthewali Gali, Chandni
Chowk (98116-02460).
Daily 9am-midnight.*
⊖ *Chandni Chowk.* ⓮

Snacks and chaat

Sultan Kullewala Kulle is a
true Delhi snack invented about
50 years ago. Today, Sultan's
grandson Sanjay sells the chaat
in a busy gali. The chaat itself is
a basket of peeled potato filled
with pomegranate seeds, boiled
chickpeas and julienned ginger,
sprinkled with homemade spice
mix. Be warned though: when
Sanjay asks you how spicy you
like your kulle, say minimum
unless you're ready for a blast.
*Cheera Khana, Roshan Pura, Nai
Sarak (2328-2848).* ⊖ *Chawri
Bazar. Mon-Sat 1-6pm.* ⓯

Sweets

Ghantewala Old Delhi boasts
several historical sweet shops,
none more famous than
Ghantewala (established in 1790)
on Chandni Chowk. Traditional
Delhi sweets available there
include the fudge-like pista
(pistachio) or kaju (cashew)
lauj and habshi halwa (brown,

Chor Bizarre

caremelised milk sweet). Or simply ask for the speciality of the season.

1862, Chandni Chowk (2328-0490). ⊖ Chandni Chowk. Daily 8am-9pm. ⑯

Special Jaleba Specialises in the art of the jaleba (the colossal cousin of the jalebi) served up on a leaf plate.

1469/1 Fountain Chowk, Chandni Chowk (98689-67612). ⊖ Chandni Chowk. Daily 9am-10pm. Meal for two ₹40. ⑰

Others

Chor Bizarre Chor Bizarre is *the* restaurant for Kashmiri food in Delhi, and always has been. The name is a play on the infamous Chor Bazaar (Thieves' Market) that used to be set up in Daryaganj, and the restaurant is packed with shiny antiques and objets d' fake art. With prior notice, they will arrange a full wazwan (a formal Kashmiri Muslim banquet which traditionally consists of 36 courses). But for a single person everything you could desire is available in one tarami (a carved copper vessel with a conical top; meat tarami ₹495, veg ₹395). It isn't just a feast, it's a ritual, and Chor Bizarre is a great secular setting in which to experience it.

Hotel Broadway, 4/15-A, Asaf Ali Road (4366-3600) Daily noon-3.30pm; 7.30-11.30pm. Meal for two ₹1,200. ⑱

Lala Dulli Chand Naresh Gupta fruit kulfi The kulfis at Dulli Chand win points for inventiveness and beauty. Almost every fruit under the sun has been given the treatment here: hollowed-out, its innards frozen into flavoured kulfi within its outer shell. The apple, for example, looks like an indigenous candy apple (₹100). Mangoes (₹100; Alfonsos ₹125), chikoos (₹50),

Dariba Kalan

oranges (₹100), even kiwis (₹80): name the fruit in season and it's in the frosty jewel-cave of a freezer. *934 Kucha Pati Ram, Bazaar Sita Ram (2323-7085).* ⊖ *Chawri Bazar. Daily noon-8pm.* ⑲

Moti Mahal Moti Mahal has been in existence since Independence, when it was transplanted from Peshawar to Daryaganj along with owner Kundan Lal Gujral. The original restaurant retains an air of having seen better days. On the menu is the silhouette of a rooster – representative of the famous butter chicken (₹195, half) reputedly invented here. Or try the much superior dal meat, hearty urad dal cooked with rich chunks of mutton, perfect to fold into lachha parathas. Like a senile blue blood, offended by the flashy new-money, Moti Mahal clearly prints on its receipt that "We have no other branch". *3704 Netaji Subhash Marg,*

Daryaganj, opposite Prince Pan (2327-3011). Daily 11am-midnight. No qawwali on Tue. No alcohol. All major credit cards. ⑳

Shopping

Aap Ki Pasand Heaven for tea connoisseurs. Sanjay Kapoor is a sommelier in his own right and his product is no less subtle. (The shop even carries a hybrid that claims a flavour like Chardonnay of the Chablis terroir.) His teas are priced between ₹60 and ₹1,600 a kilo, the finest being the President's Tea, a Darjeeling first flush (the best tea in the world if you had to pick one). *Sterling House, 15 Netaji Subhash Marg, Daryaganj (2326-0373) Daily 9.30am-7pm, Sunday closed.* ㉑

Chattah Chowk Delhi's first modern shopping mall might have been Ansal Plaza (built 1999) but the essential principles of the mall

Old Delhi

were put in place in the Chattah Chowk of Shahjahanabad, the first covered market in Hindustan. Vendors still sell practically everything – embroidered prayer caps, brass utensils, very-crimson velvety cloth for sofa covers, even glitzy, sequinned burqas. The shops along the rear specialise in pillows, mattresses and quilts. You can buy a blanket, complete with a bright soft-sheened cover, for just ₹400. A walk through the bazaar is not for the faint-hearted. The lanes are narrow, the shopkeepers and customers loud, and the men can get impolite. But if you brave all this, Chattah Chowk is worth visiting for its antique charm and for the history that still clings to the name. *Red Fort. ⊖ Chandni Chowk.* ㉒

Dariba Kalan This narrow lane gets its name from the Persian phrase dur-e be-baha, which means pearl without comparison. It is said that it was once lined

with shops selling precious stones, gems, gold and silver, armloads of which would go to the harem quarters of Emperor Shah Jahan. For the modern day visitor, it is easy to miss the ancient jewellers' street – the municipal sign is buried under jute sacking. Look out for the ancient jalebiwala at the corner of the left turn just before Gurdwara Sis Ganj on Chandni Chowk.

Most of the shops on Dariba Kalan now sell jewellery in contemporary designs, but there are hidden treasures in the shadows; an antique silver-framed mirror, or a 200-year-old coin studded in a chunky silver ring. The only thing a visitor needs to take to Dariba Kalan (apart from cash – only a few shops accept credit cards) is time and patience. *Dariba Kalan, Chandni Chowk, near Gurudwara Sis Ganj.* ㉓

Gulabsingh Johrimal ittar

There is a small bottle on his shelves that Krishna Mohan Singh, the sixth-generation owner of the perfumery, treasures. It contains a few inches of an emerald green fluid that sells at ₹720 for 10ml. This is ruh khus ittar (soul of vetiver perfume). Ittar is fragrance for true connoisseurs, and ayurveda acknowledges vetiver as a cooling agent and its fragrance as an aroma that builds harmony between body and mind. The ruh gulab (soul of the rose), at ₹10,000 for 10ml, is the most expensive ittar in the city. *320 Dariba Kalan (2327-1345). Daily 10.30am-7.30pm. All credit cards accepted. Also at 467,*

The Khari Baoli spice market

DELHI BY AREA

New Gramophone House

Chandni Chowk, (2326-3743). Daily 10.30am-7.30pm. All credit cards. ☻ *Chandni Chowk for both locations.* ㉔

Khari Baoli It is not considered impolite to sneeze as you walk around this seventeenth-century spice market. A good sinus-clearing snort is meant to be the mark of pure spices. If Khari Baoli could be distilled into a perfume, the mingled aroma of cloves, cinnamon, bay leaves, star anise, punctuated with sweet notes of raisins, cashew, chironji and almonds and topped with herbal hints of the ashwagandha, is what would be in the bottle. Visit after lunch, when the market empties out a little. Prices fluctuate by the day, but bargaining is discouraged. Make sure you exit the way you came in, because the other end of Khari Baoli market opens out into the GB Road (the city's main red-light district, among

other things). *Khari Baoli, Chandni Chowk.* ☻ *Chandni Chowk. 10am-7pm. Best day to visit Saturday.* ㉕

New Gramophone House
Opened in Lahore in 1930, the NGH relocated after Partition to this spot, where the Rajpals were granted resettlement space. Today the building is typically decrepit, and you enter through a shop downstairs that sells cheap shoes. You can buy LPs of old Bollywood films for under ₹100 and they have a modest selection of Western music. They even have some obscure avant-garde jazz titles, by the likes of Cecil Taylor, which you can snap up for ₹100 a pop. If you love old things, you might also want to pick yourself up a working wind-up gramophone (₹2,500). *31B Pleasure Garden Market, first floor, Chandni Chowk (2327-1524).* ☻ *Chandni Chowk. Mon-Sat 11am-9pm.* ㉖

DELHI BY AREA

Central Delhi

Jantar Mantar

Raisina Hill

THE CAPITAL

The modern half of Delhi owes its existence to the British.
The city designed by Sir Edwin Lutyens became the eighth
imperial bastion in Delhi, following seven that had been
constructed, fortified, besieged, destroyed and often rebuilt.
At the end of the nineteenth century, after the final defeat of the
Mughals, Delhi was a shrunken post-Imperial capital, clustered
around the Old City of Shahjahanabad. Everything south of there
was open fields and villages, interspersed with the ruins and
remainders of even earlier imperial capitals.

When the British Raj moved its capital from Calcutta to Delhi,
in 1911, Sir Edwin Lutyens was commissioned to build the new
city in this hilly plain south of the Old City. That's how central
Delhi, with its wide, tree-lined avenues and over-imposing
imperial architecture, came to exist. Today it's the seat of
India's political power, with the Parliament, the Secretariat,
most ministries and the President's House.

Today, however, central Delhi is no longer synonymous with
executive power. This is the part of town with the most theatres,
art galleries and music auditoria, great temples and gurudwaras,
and lots of shopping. Connaught Place, the three concentric
circles of collonaded shopping arcades at the geographic heart of
Delhi, is also the civic heart of Delhi. It's an area that's getting
more vibrant by the day, thanks to its being the central-most
junction of the Delhi Metro. No trip to Delhi has even begun
without doing the rounds of CP's shopping and restaurants.

LIVE MET SMART

Welcome to THE MET - the future of hospitality. Innovative design, modern technology and eco-friendly practices have been enhanced with new ideas and bright insights. Enjoy luxury with a conscience at our smart new avatar.

SAKURA
JAPANESE CUISINE

chutney
bar + tandoor
INDIAN CUISINE

ZING
WORLD CUISINE

CRAFT HOUSE
CLUSIVE LIFESTYLE STORE

THE METROPOLITAN HOTEL

Bangla Sahib Road, New Delhi - 110001, INDIA
T : +91 11 42500200 E: info@hotelmetdelhi.com
www.hotelmetdelhi.com

Sights & Museums

Agrasen ki Baoli

One of the most celebrated photographs shot in Delhi is Raghu Rai's image of a man throwing himself into the deep water of Agrasen's baoli, or step-well. Delhi's numerous baolis are in a sorry condition today, neglected after falling water-tables left them dry. But the baoli of Maharaja Agrasen, though it has been dry since the last decade, is still breath-taking. As its deep, intricately-cut maw sinks down ahead of you, the towers of Connaught Place shoot into the sky in the background, with an effect that's practically like an Escher painting.
Hailey Road, Connaught Place.
⊖ *Barakhamba Road* ❶

Bangla Sahib

Agrasen ki baoli

Bangla Sahib Gurdwara

It's fair to say that the golden dome of Bangla Sahib Gurdwara marks the spiritual heart of New Delhi. The Hanuman Mandir and the Sacred Heart Cathedral cluster around it. It was built in 1783, as the bungalow (thus "bangla") of Mirza Raja Jai Singh, a commander under the Mughal emperor Aurangzeb. Guru Har Kishan, the eight Sikh guru, lived with Jai Singh, and is said to have tended to victims of a smallpox epidemic and later died of the illness here. Today visitors of all religions visit the gurdwara, and headscarves are lent to to anyone without one. A beautiful sarovar, a holy pond, fills the main courtyard. Behind it is the prayer hall, which holds the Sikh holy book called the Granth Sahib; enter after washing your feet at

DELHI BY AREA

Birla Mandir

the taps. The granthi (priest) reads from the book and the soothing chants are heard all day long along with the gurbani (hymns). All those who visit are given a portion of the sweet halwa as a prasad and are welcome to partake of the free langar meals.

By Gol Dak Khana, intersection of Baba Kharak Singh Marg and Ashok Roads. Daily 24 hours. ❷

Bhairon Mandir

Clinging to the ramparts of the Old Fort, Bhairon Mandir is a one-of-a-kind Hindu shrine that accepts liquor as prasad. A signboard outside, warning devotees not to give it to beggars, is mostly ignored. At the Mandir, the tradition is to offer some of the whiskey (or beer, vodka, rum…) to the deity, and the rest to the priest to take home. Bhairon Baba, a demon killed by Durga but absolved of all sins during his dying moments, attracts the biggest crowd on Sundays. The sweeper claims to collect more than a thousand bottles the mornings after. An offering of meat is also acceptable, according to a priest, and it's not unusual to proffer live chickens.

Near Pragati Maidan parking, opposite Gate No 2. ⊖ *Pragati Maidan* ❸

Birla Mandir

No one really calls this temple by its real name: Lakshmi Narayan Mandir. Instead it is the Birla Mandir, after the familiar name of the freedom-movement-era industrialist who built it. According to city lore, the work never stops at Birla Mandir, because of superstitions that the family's fortunes would decline once construction ended. The temple hosts massive celebrations at all major Hindu festivals; the biggest is Janmashtami, to celebrate the birth of Krishna.

The temple is dedicated to Vishnu and is said to be inspired by the architecture of the ancient temples of Orissa.
Mandir Marg, Gol Market (2336-3637). ⊖ *Jhandewalan.* ❹

Crafts Museum

Officially known as the National Handicrafts and Handloom Museum, this is one of the city's most charming museums. Tucked into a leafy plot right across the road from the Old Fort and the National Stadium, it's a treasure trove of textiles, pottery and other vibrant handicraft traditions from across the country. Award-winning craftmen hold workshops in the recreated mud huts, and let you have a go at the loom or the potters' wheel. The museum shop is a good place for souvenirs.
Bhairon Road, near Pragati Maidan (2337-1887). ⊖ *Pragati Maidan. Open Tue-Sun 10am-5.30pm. Entry free. Guided tours for groups on request only.* ❺

Crafts Museum

Dargah Shah-e-Mardan

Dargah Shah-e-Mardan

At the beginning of Muharram every year, thousands of Delhi Muslims walk to Karbala. Not the original Karbala in central Iraq, but the open field south of Lodhi Road, next to the sprawling Dargah Shah-e-Mardan. This dargah is the largest of Delhi's imambargahs, gathering-places where Shias mourn the death of Imam Hussain ibn Ali, the grandson of the Prophet, at the battle of Karbala (Iraq). This isn't the violent matam procession that Shias conduct in Old Delhi, lashing themselves bloody with leather lashes or bundles of nails. At Karbala things are more festive, as devotees bury taziyas, tableau-replicas of the tomb of Hussain, built from wood, fabric, paper and flowers. The rest of the year, the dargah Shah-e-Mardan is utterly serene, allowing you to appreciate its religious artefacts,

like a footprint supposed to belong to Hazrat Ali.
Near Karbala Grounds, Lodhi Colony. ⊖ *Jor Bagh* ⑥

Delhi Metro Museum

The large Patel Chowk Metro station doubles as the museum of the Delhi Metro, every Dilliwala's pride and joy. Two long rows of of displays illuminate the construction and operation of

Delhi Metro Museum

the Metro, through charming exhibitions like deep-soil samples from different quarters of the city. There's a complete section on the building of the Chawri Bazaar station – the world's second deepest. Not a train freak? Not to worry. Pick up a Metro tie, key-chain or a miniature model of the rolling stock instead.

⊖ *Patel Chowk. Tue-Sun 10am-4pm.* ❼

Eternal Gandhi Museum

The Eternal Gandhi Multimedia Museum has the difficult task of having to work with ponderous history and still reverse the general impression of Indian museums – tatty, impersonal and boring. Located on the first floor of the larger and blander Gandhi Smriti Musuem, the first exhibit is a set of oddly-shaped installations called "hyper-instruments". Speaking into their mouths has varying effects – some sing back

strains from hymns that were Gandhi's favourites, others translate your voice into harp-like music. Move from a model of Gandhi's jail cell, complete with interactive prison rods, to the Corridor of Interfaith Unity, and you'll appreciate the ingenuity of the enterprise is striking.

5, Tees January Marg (3095-7269). Tue-Sun (except second Saturday of each month) 10am-5pm. ❽

Hanuman Mandir

Hanuman, the monkey-like god devoted to Rama, is easily one of Delhi's favourite gods: observe the gargantuan statue of him looming over the Metro line near Jhandewalan. At the Hanuman Mandir, size is not everything, though. This temple's deity is Bala Hanuman – the monkey god as a child. Devotees throng to the place on Tuesdays and Saturdays. The mandir is the centre of a

Eternal Gandhi Museum

Get the local experience

Over 50 of the world's top destinations available.

high-energy, monkey-infested market, churning with food stalls, computer-toting astrologers, palmists, bangle-sellers, mehendiwalis (henna artists) and other stalls selling temple paraphernalia, incense and marigolds. Funnily, though hanuman was a celibate, the festive market outside this temple is most popular with women, especially brides to be. The covered shacks are lined with bright jewel-coloured bangles. The chudiwalas (bangle-sellers) of this bangle market on Baba Kharak Singh Marg claim to have been around for over 300 years. *Baba Kharak Singh Marg, next to Rivoli Cinema.* ❾

India Gate

Delhi's most iconic building from the modern era, India Gate has a rather grandiose purpose – a memorial to British and Indian

India Gate

Jantar Mantar

DELHI BY AREA

soldiers killed in World War I – and a more humble reality. To most Dilliwalas, India Gate means family picnics with balloons and ice cream. Yet the memorial to the Unknown Soldier remains poignant, and the upturned rifle and helmet evoke patriotic sentiments even today. The Amar Jawan Jyoti, or the flame of the immortal solder, was added in 1971 and burns night and day. *On Rajpath.* ❿

Jantar Mantar

The phrase Jantar Mantar means one thing to Dilliwalas today – political protest. This ancient observatory, now on the road leading to Parliament, is the designated zone for expressing dissent to the State. Three hundred years ago, though, this was an empty plain where the Mughal and Rajput astronomers studied the gears of the universe.

Central Delhi

Originally called the Yantra Mantra ("devices of formulation"), the four massive instruments determined the time of day and helped produce star charts. The Planetarium periodically holds viewings of astral alignments. *Parliament Street. Daily 9am-7pm. Indian nationals ₹5, others ₹100.* ⊖ *Rajiv Chowk.* ⑪

Lodhi Gardens

One of the best decisions made by the planners of New Delhi was to lay this large park around the mausolea left by the Lodhi and Sayyid kings, the final Sultanate dynasties of the 15th and 16th centuries, which yielded to the great Mughals. Today, the Lodhi Gardens is one of the great

The Lodhi Gardens

National Museum

equalising spaces of Delhi, where cabinet ministers have to step around shop-boys as they take a morning speed-walk. Arguably Delhi's most friendly and social park area, the Lodhi Gardens stay open past sundown, when the park clears out a little, and spotlights brilliantly illuminate the tombs.
Enter from Lodhi Road or Max Mueller Marg. Open daily 5am-8pm. Entry free. ⑫

National Museum

The National Museum Institute of the History of Art, Conservation and Museology is one vast diorama of Indian civilization. Its massive collection ranges from pre-historic archeology to contemporary tribal and folk art and objects. It has a collection of 800 ancient sculptures across the ages. The museums displays artifacts found during excavations or those that have fallen off the main structures, such as carvings and statues from temple compounds.
Maulana Azad Road, Janpath (2301-8415) Tuesday-Sunday 10am-5pm. Entry Indian citizens ₹10, others ₹300, students ₹1. Camera charges extra. Audio tour available in English, French, German, Japanese and Hindi. ⑬

Nehru Planetarium

It's a planetarium, so you know what to expect: cosmic projection on the domed ceiling and walls, super-flexible seats that go all the way back, an incantatory narration that plunges you into the realm of planets, constellations and space travel. But the creaky Nehru Planetarium just underwent a major revamp, installing a hybrid projection machine that promises "inspired star field views" and "a full-dome immersive digital experience". In an age of IMAX and 4-D cinemas, it's great to know that a few rupees will buy you back your childhood oohs and aahs. Pop upstairs

World Class

Perfect places to stay, eat and explore.

TIME OUT GUIDES
WRITTEN BY
LOCAL EXPERTS
visit timeout.com/shop

afterward for a hot coffee and potato patty to bring you back to earth.

Teen Murti Bhavan, Teen Murti Marg (2301-4504, 2301-6350). Open Tue-Sun 11.30am-4pm. Entry price subject to change. ⑬

Parliament Museum

This is surely one of the most aesthetically radical public institutions in India. Mudane themes like national integration and the drafting of the constitution are illustrated with violent colours and surreal dioramas. Be warned: you may leave thinking that India, prior to 1950, was populated by mannequins. The leader of Mannequindia is an animatronic Nehru, who will single you out with a waxy finger and delivers his tryst-with-destiny speech from a champing jaw. Visitors to the Parliament Museum are bullied by their guide into singing songs, as they're projected into a video of Gandhi's Dandi March. Other exhibits in the Parliament Museum display Stone Age people, which might be a snarky comment on Indian parliamentarians.

Parliament Library, Pandit Pant Marg, opp. Rakab Gunj Gurdwara (2303-5318, 2303-5325). ⊖Patel Chowk. Tue-Sat 11am-5.30pm. Entry ₹10. ⑮

Purana Qila

Purana Qila, or the Old Fort, is a place heavy with legends. Some believe this was the site of ancient Indraprastha, the capital of the Pandava heros in the epic Mahabharata. Others just believe that it's haunted. Archaeological digs have turned up coins and earthenware from 200 BC. History records that it served as the principal fort and residence of Sher Shah Suri, who briefly ejected the Mughals from Delhi in the sixteenth century. When they

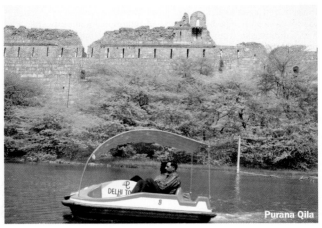

Purana Qila

Sacred Heart Cathedral

returned, it was home to the emperor Humayun, who fell to his death there, descending from his library. Enter through the massive Bara Darwaza and walk paths winding through lawns and flowerbeds. Watch for the Qila-I-Kuna mosque and the Sher Mandal, a two-storey octagonal tower of red sandstone. If the idea of taking out a pedal-boat for a half hour strikes your fancy, go onto the moat and see the fort ramparts from a different angle at every turn.

Mathura Road, near Delhi Zoo. ⊖ Pragati Maidan. Open daily 10am-5pm. Admission free. Mathura Road, near Pragati Maidan. Entry Indian adults ₹5, others ₹100. Children under 15 enter free. ⑯

Sacred Heart Cathedral

It's still the dream of Catholic brides in the city to be married at the grand church with its towering curved roof, polished stone floors and magnificent marble altar. Established in 1929, the Sacred Heart Cathedral is one of the most popular Roman Catholic churches in the city, as well as the mother-church of the Archdiocese of Delhi. The cathedral was designed by architect Henry Medd, whose proposal was chosen by a panel of judges including Edward Lutyens (who approved of its clear European architectural influences, of columns and high arches). The ochre brick finish has an old-world charm and is brightly lit up on Easter and Christmas.

1 Ashoka Place, Gol Dak Khana (2336-3593). English Mass: 6:30am & 6pm. ⑰

The Zoo

The National Zoological Park was opened to the public in 1959, presenting Delhi residents with 176 acres of lawns, animal enclosures and woodland,

interspersed with brooks and lakes that attract thriving populations of migratory birds. It's all tucked in around the ruins of the Old Fort. The zoo has rare animals including a pair of the rare Hoolock gibbons (*Hoolock hoolock*), India's only ape, and there's always a special excitement around the lions and the white tigers. In fact, the Zoo attracts Delhi families from such a variety of backgrounds, it deserves mention as a fine place to watch the human species as well. The authorities recently installed a souvenir shop, modern cloakrooms and an ATM.
Mathura Road, next to Purana Qila (2435-9825). Open Sat-Thur 9am-4.30pm. Entry: Indian adults ₹10, foreigners ₹50, children below 5 free. ⑱

STADIA Indira Gandhi Sports Complex
This stadium is the Common-wealth Games venue for cycling (track), artistic and rhythmic gymnastics and wrestling.
✆ *Indraprastha.* ⑲

Major Dhyan Chand National Stadium
Hockey.
✆ *Pragati Maidan.* ⑳

Dr SP Mukherjee Swimming Complex
Diving, swimming, synchronised swimming.
✆ *Ramakrishna Mission Marg; Patel Chowk.* ㉑

Talkatora Indoor Stadium
Boxing.
✆ *Ramakrishna Mission Marg; Patel Chowk.* ㉒

Eating & Drinking

Amici
Andrea Aftab Pauro's restaurant lives up to its name, which means "friends". Amici serves toned-down Italian style food, with an emphasis on wood-fired pizzas. Its clean, pale interiors are very conducive to gossipy lunches or

DELHI BY AREA

The Zoo

Amici

Andhra Bhavan

Technically the staff cafeteria attached to the state house of Andhra Pradesh, a southern Indian state, Andhra Bhavan has become so popular, it's now being called overrated. But it's still one of Delhi's ten most definitive eating experiences. The set-up couldn't be more basic: plastic chairs and tables, and hyper-efficient staff that scurry about with pails full of various dishes. Order a thali (₹60), add on a meat dish (chicken or mutton, in a spicy fry or curry; ₹50) and an order of chicken biryani (₹90). Find a chair and it won't be two seconds before you're blinking at the mountain of food in front of you. This is not a place to linger over your meal. Finish off and grab a sweet paan (₹5) on your way out.

AP Bhawan, 1 Ashoka Road (2338-7499). Daily 7:30-10am; noon-3pm; 7:30-10pm. Meal for two ₹300. ㉔

chatty afternoons over coffee. Desserts are a high point, and the boozy tiramisu in a tumbler is a must-try.

47, Middle Lane, Khan Market (4358-7191). Daily 11am-11pm. Meal for two ₹1,600. ㉓

The thali at Andhra Bhavan

Blanco

This chic café is open all day, but lunch is the best time to enjoy the cheerful outdoors section and the large windows that flood the small white space with sunlight. The extensive menu bears the mark of food consultants Suddha Kukreja & Manav Sharma. The choices meander from Malaysian-style banana-wrapped fish to California-style maki rolls. Try the kingfish steak and the crispy red-snapper salad with Vietnamese pineapple salsa. For dessert don't miss the classic Philly cheesecake. *62, Khan Market (4359-7155). Daily noon-11pm. Meal for two ₹3,000.* ㉕

Delhi Parsi Anjuman

The Parsis – Zoroastrians refugees who arrived from Persia centuries ago – have a tiny community in Delhi. The Anjuman is a resthouse that has the only agiary (fire temple) in the city, and it's also the only place in Delhi that serves authentic Parsi cuisine. Manager and chef Dhun Bagli cooks up a fixed Parsi menu for lunch and dinner everyday, with the specials of patra-ni-machi (fish filets anointed with a coconut-based marinade and steamed in banana leaves), dhansak (mixed lentils and meat cooked together with light spices), and salli murgi (spicy chicken curry served garnished with potato straws) on Sunday and Friday. The only condition is that you reserve a table by 10am so Bagli can expect you. *Delhi Parsi Dharamshala, near the Maulana Azad Medical College gates, Bahadurshah Zafar Marg (2323-8615). Daily 1-2.30pm, 8-10pm. Cash only. Meal for two ₹400.* ㉖

Khan Chacha

Very few establishments anywhere in the world have the kind of following that Khan Chacha's hole-in-the-wall

commanded in Delhi, until he was shut down in 2009. Naturally he reopened in a larger hole in Khan Market soon afterward, not before it became cool to proclaim an allegiance to nearby Saleem's. Yet there's little dispute that Khan Chacha is the czar of the beloved chicken tikka-roomali roll (₹75). His mutton, paneer and occasional fish offerings are also all slapped and coated with that familiar red spice mixture, perfectly charred, then wrapped at lightning speed with a bundle of onions and a splash of fresh green chutney in a floury roomali roti.
50 Middle Lane, Khan Market (98106-71103). Daily noon-11pm. Meal for two ₹150. 🐵

Latitude

This warm, lazy place is perfect for a lunch date. Chef Ritu Dalmia's menu is capable and friendly, encompassing various Mediterranean cuisines. The traditional-style fishcakes and the spinach & Gorgonzola flan are a must-try. The Arabic bread grilled with halloumi cheese and sprinkled with chilly flakes and za'atar is good too. Make sure you save room for the day's dessert.
9 Khan Market (2464-7175). Daily 11am-11pm. Meal for two ₹2,000. 🐵

Lodi-The Garden Restaurant

Right by the heart of Delhi's lush Lodhi Gardens, this is a beautiful place to grab a drink. The outdoor seating area is a winner, with wrought-iron furniture and mood lighting. The inside looks like a mountain lodge and there's a nice balcony under a canopy of trees upstairs. Stop by on a stroll through Lodhi Gardens, especially if there's a live music act on. It's also a great place to take the kids. They can kick off their shoes, run around, swing on the jhoolas (swings), roll on the grass and pick the special menu of fish and chips – while you enjoy your fine

Khan Chacha

Lodi-The Garden Restaurant

Mamagoto

Mediterranean meal.
Lodhi Road, opposite Mausam Bhavan (2465-2808). Daily noon-3pm, 7-11pm. Meal for two ₹3,000. 🟤

Mamagoto

"Mamagoto" means "play with your food" and it is evident that someone had a lot of fun playing around with food and design at this Khan Market eatery. The walls are illustrated with cartoon pandas and girls in Mao suits, and their chopsticks come with instructions on how to achieve the "Walrus Face" look. The flavours of China, Thailand and Japan hop through the food in the form of lemongrass, ginger, galangal, coconut and Thai basil. Try the fish filet in pepper sauce (₹275) which melts in your mouth, while staying crisp on the edges.
53, Middle Lane, first floor, Khan Market (4516-6060). Daily noon-11pm. Meal for two ₹900. 🟤

Mian Babu Khan

Epicurean wishes are granted at the foot of the hillock that houses the mazaar of pir Sheikh Abu Bakr Tulshi Haideri Kalandari Rahmatullah. Offerings are made to the pir in matkas (clay pots) which are then hung upside-down on the keekar trees.

The matkas are also an advertisement for one of the best biryanis in the city. At the base of the dargah, and next to a garage, is the kitchen of Babu Khan. Sold only as takeaway on a first-come-first-served basis, Khan's biryani (chicken or mutton) and the qorma have a congregation of faithful devotees. Cooked in dum-style, the fragrant biryani has tender meat ready to fall of the bone, while the qorma hums with the warmth of its slow-roasted masala. He also has roomali roti and galauti kababs to munch on while you wait for the main course to be packed.

Time Out

timeout.com/travel
Get the local experience

Camel racing in the United Arab Emirates

© Bernardino Testa/iTP Images

Babu Khan's Dhaba, Matka Peer, near Pragati Maidan gate number 3, next to petrol station, Dargah Matke Pir (2337-1454). ⊖ Pragati Maidan. Daily 9am-8pm. Take away orders only. Cash only. Meal for two ₹150 ㉛

Naoki

The kaiseki counter at The Aman New Delhi features chef Naoki Okumura's signature "French kaiseki" cuisine. Kaiseki is the Japanese equivalent of a multi-course French degustation meal. Chef Okumura serves it all in small plates so that you can sample bites of several different things. Though you may be left broke and wanting more, a Naoki meal is a feast of tiny offerings. *Aman New Delhi, Lodhi Road (4363-3333). Daily noon-3pm, 6.30-11pm. Lunch for two ₹10,000 (dinner is more).* ㉜

Parikrama

High over Connaught Place is a revolving restaurant with an astonishing view over Delhi. Parikrama is the centre-point of a circle that encloses the Jama Masjid, the Bangla Sahib Gurudwara, Jantar Mantar and the President's House. The Ridge and the Yamuna are tangents on either horizon. For 20 years,

Parikrama

Tapas Bar at The Lodhi

Parikrama has had a semi-secret existence, guaranteed by its truly awful food. But in 2009, things were turned around. The shabby '70s air – which we love – still hangs heavily on it, but the food is much improved. You can kill a lot of time with the Murg Kebab "Parikrama" (₹360), a mildly spiced chicken tikka, and Kingfisher beer (₹225). It's really just a pretext to stay seated for the 100 minutes it takes you to be whirled around 360 degrees. *Antariksh Bhawan, 22 Kasturba Gandhi Marg (2372-1616). Daily 12.30-11pm, happy hours 4-7pm. Major credit cards accepted. Meal for two ₹2,000.* ③

Ploof

The nice thing about this Lodhi Colony mainstay is that you can visit for an unpretentiously elegant meal – lobster and Alaskan king crab feature on its seafood-centric menu – and also stop by for a light casual meal that won't break the bank. The service here is another plus. Try the platter of oriental tapas and

the chicken steak with celery-mashed potatoes and lemongrass. *13 Main Market, Lodhi Colony (2464-9026) Daily 11.30am-3.30pm; 7-11pm. Meal for two ₹2,500.* ③

Tapas Bar at The Lodhi

The Lodhi's bar – a long vertical room with a kitted-out wine cellar towards one end – is an elegant affair, warmly inviting and buzzing with activity. The tapas platter features a few delicious anchovies, a couple of mussels and a few thin slices of a pungent chorizo, all drizzled with olive oil. Our favourite order is the grilled tuna with paprika, asparagus and chorizo, two gorgeous cuts of piscine goodness, making you feel like you can taste the sea (no small feat in Delhi). The pomegranate sangria (all cocktails ₹750) is superlative. *Aman New Delhi, Lodhi Road (4363-3333) Daily 7pm- 1am. Meal for two ₹5,000.* ③

threesixty°

Sample the a la carte sushi menu

with its lovely array of sashimi, maki rolls and non-seafood options; or try it all with one of the platters. We especially like one of the Chef's signature rolls: rainbow maki (California roll wrapped with salmon, tuna and whitefish). Sushi also makes a good appetiser, especially if you plan on trying the main menu's yakitori options. The bento boxes, Japanese soups, teppanyaki and yakitori are variably also on their lunch buffet. Keep in mind that the sushi chef leaves at 10.30pm.

Oberoi Hotel, *Dr Zakir Hussein Marg (2430-4360). Daily 12.30pm-3pm, 7pm-12.30am. Meal for two ₹3,500.* ⊛

Triveni Tea Terrace

The café atop the Triveni Kala Sangam serves up delicious home-styled Indian food in a relaxed environment. The sunny patio is festooned with green creepers and is the perfect backdrop to their potato parathas. The café, run by Mina Singh, has exhaustive menus for breakfast, lunch and dinner. Don't miss the masala omlette with toast for breakfast and keema mattar (mutton mince and peas) for lunch.

Triveni Kala Sangam, *205 Tansen Marg (98101-18115) Daily 10.30am-6.30pm. Meal for two ₹500.* ⊛

Eating & drinking in Connaught Place

Cibo

Past the staid façade of Hotel Janpath stand carved gates that open onto another world: gold statuary, a dramatic centrepiece of gold grapes clustering around an almost-hidden fountain, cascading waterfalls and a never-ending courtyard. The décor is heavy on gilt and grandeur, but with deft touches like the antique-style tiles and wire-hung light-bulbs above the central island-bar. Try the calamari fritters (₹650) and the shrimp ravioli (₹525).

Triveni Tea Terrace

India Coffee House

Allergic to shellfish? Stick to the wine.

Hotel Janpath, Janpath (4302-9291). Daily lunch noon-3pm, dinner 7-11.30pm. All major credit cards. Meal for two ₹5,000. ⃣

India Coffee House

From feeding bored US Marines during World War II to sustaining the socialist intelligentsia through the '60s, the India Coffee House has has a career more than colourful enough to make up for its plain appearance. A huge, airy terrace, cheap food, top-notch Indian coffee, clattering fans – its a bit of a time portal in the middle of the rapidly McDonaldsising Connaught Place. Waiters in baggy all-whites and "bearer" caps serve up greasy but great-tasting food (try the mutton chops or mutton dosa) and filter coffee for as little as ₹8.

Mohan Singh Place, second floor, Connaught Place (2334-2994). Daily 9am-9pm. Meal for two ₹200. ⃣

Q'BA

Taking up an entire corner of a Connaught Place block, Q'BA's main attraction is lovely park-facing balcony that looks out over

Chowk. Daily noon–midnight. All credit cards accepted. Meal for two ₹3,000. ⑩

Sancho's

Despite some Punjabification, Sancho's can lay out a spread of chilli con carne nachos, buffalo tacos and a margharita that's just as mixed-up, messy and irresistable as American tex-mex itself. *M-48, Connaught Place, opposite Shankar Market (4308-4656). ⊖ Rajiv Chowk. Daily noon-midnight. Alcohol served only on Fridays and Saturdays.* ㊶

Saravana Bhavan

Sarvana Bhavan is both a typical south Indian "Udupi" joint (think light vegetarian snacks like dosas), but also a branch of a mega-franchise with 27 outlets nationally and 30 worldwide. The Connaught Place outlet, long famed for having the best sambar in town, is where many Delhi Tamilians go out for a meal. The

Central Park. They dish out competent continental and above-average Indian food. Reserve a park-facing table at sunset and dive into a faultless mojito. *E 42-43, Connaught Place, Inner Circle (4151-2888). ⊖ Rajiv*

DELHI BY AREA

Baba Kharak Singh Marg

local legend is that when Hotel Saravana Bhavan opened a few doors down from McDonald's, the queues under the Golden Arches marched straight over to the SB Lotus-bud. Today Janpath, tomorrow the world.
46, Janpath (2331-7755, 5535-4405). ✆ *Rajiv Chowk. Daily 8am-10.30pm. Meal for two ₹300.* ⓒ

Wenger's

Everyone's favourite pastry shop has been around for 84 years in the hub of Central Delhi. Opened by a South African waitress Ms Wenger in 1926, it is currently in the capable hands of Atul Tandon and family. The shop sells fantastic cakes, pastries, breads, chocolates, cookies and other delights for the sweet-toothed. Among the wide range of Swiss confectionary, the fudge is delectable.
A-16, Inner Circle Connaught Place (2332-4373). ✆ *Rajiv Chowk. Daily 10am-8pm.* ⑬

Shopping

Baba Kharak Singh Marg

State emporia – official outlets selling heritage handicrafts from Indian states – have long been a Delhi-winter afternoon hangout. Be prepared to do some serious walking and shopping. The West Bengal emporium has lovely Bengali saris in silk and cotton. Gurjari, Gujarat's state emporium, is a riot of colours, on bags and jewellery, stationery and fabrics. Further down the street Purbasha, the Tripura emporium, has great cane furniture. Lepakshi, the Andhra Pradesh emporium, has beautiful gold jewellery on the ground floor, and a wide range of cotton fabric on the second floor. Next door is Kairali, the Kerala emporium which sells temple and church velakkus (lamps), as well as saris. That's just the tip of the iceberg.
Baba Kharak Singh Marg, near Hanuman Mandir. Mon-Sat 10am-7pm. ⑭

Mehar Chand Market

This rapidly gentrifying market is Lodhi Road's cool artery, running between the Habitat Center and a cluster of mechanic shops by the Ring Railroad. This street is home to a cool new crop of shops teeming with gorgeous textiles, hard-to-find books and quirky household accessories. Its flagship store is **CMYK**, an art and design-focused bookshop. Named for cyan, magenta, yellow and key (black), the pigments used in colour printing, it's appropriately colourful, and also sleek, friendly and Wi-Fi enabled. CMYK will even give you a cup of coffee while you read, which says a lot about the niche they opted for. There's also the block-printed textiles at **Soma**, more eco-conscious textiles at **Ratan Textiles**, the goofy, cult t-shirt brand **Tantra** and the kitschy little gift emporium **Crazy Daisy**. CMYK *15-16 Mehar Chand Market, Lodhi Road (2464-1881).*
Daily 9.30am-8.30pm. ㊺
Crazy Daisy *24 Mehar Chand Market (4607-6566).* ㊻
Ratan Textiles, *21-22 Mehar Chand Market.* ㊼
Soma *46-47 Mehar Chand Market (2462-7046).* ㊽
Tantra *12 Mehar Chand Market (2464-3747).* ㊾

The Book Shop

Dilliwalas have many allegiances where bookstores are concerned, but there's little dispute that The Book Shop is a cut apart. Visit for books in limited editions that you're unable to find elsewhere. *13/7 Jor Bagh Market (2469-7102). Mon-Sat 10.30am-7pm.* ㊿

Khan Market

The position of Khan Market in the lives of Delhi's elite is deep and sentimental. Once a refined but sleepy market, it is now the priciest real estate in the city, and has a clientele to match. Khan Market is full of excellent restau-

Central Delhi

rants (see Eating & drinking) but not too many unmissable shops. Among the neat shops are the **Bahri Sons** bookshop, **FabIndia** (see p172) and **Forest Essentials**, which uses cold-pressed oils in high-quality body products. Then there's **Good Earth**, which sells uniformly gorgeous home products at uniformly nerve-wracking prices (but is really worth walking around). Ultimately, "Khan" is not a market as much as an idea of the good life in Delhi, and reflects that transforming idea well.

Bahri Sons *Opposite main gate (2469-4610). Mon-Sat 10.30am-2pm, 3pm-7.30pm.* ⑤

FabIndia *Central Hall, above shop no. 20 and 21 (4368-3100). Daily 11am-8pm. Also see p172.* ②

Forest Essentials *B-46 (4175-7057). Daily 10.30am-9pm.* ③

Good Earth *No 9, front lane (2464-7175). Daily 11am-7pm.* ③

Santushti

One of the classiest and most central shopping jaunts in town, Santushti is made for hours of browsing. Spread over gardens with meandering walkways, each store proffers all sorts of lovely goodies. You'll find Indian designers (like Rajesh Pratap, the uncrowned king of Indian minimal), décor, jewelry, shawls, even cigars.

Santushti Shopping Arcade, Race Course Road (2410-2724). Mon-Sat 10am-7pm. ⑤

Sunder Nagar

The Sunder Nagar market exudes a sense of genteel equilibrium. Delhi's transformation and official experiments with cityscaping have never ruffled its 50-year-old facade. Sixteen of the city's oldest and most admired jewellery houses are lined up along the

Good Earth in Khan Market

D.Minsen & Co

quad, from where they service the lifestyles of the visiting rich and famous. And it's been that way for decades: Moti Jewels' "wall of fame" features Jackie Kennedy, Gregory Peck and George Pompidou grinning at their glittering purchases.
Various jewellers and gem-shops, 11am-6.30pm. Visit Moti Jewels Palace (2435-8000) and Mayur Jewellers (2435-8664). ⓢ

Shopping in Connaught Place

D.Minsen & Co
Want to get custom-fitted riding boots made? Established in 1937, D. Minsen & Co is famous throughout India for its "Chinese shoes" and their workmanship, comfort and attention to detail. Their international reputation as a top manufacturer of customised polo boots has also been growing since the '90s with the Indian national polo team, the Argentinean polo team and the US Army polo team among the clients who swear by their knee-high leathers.
F-17 Connaught Place (4152-3520). ⊖ *Rajiv Chowk. Mon-Sat 11am-7.30pm.* ⓢ

Khadi Gram Udyog
The main stock of this government-run emporium in Connaught Place is fabric and prêt-a-porter traditional clothing made from khadi (the rough-spun cotton that Mahatma Gandhi turned into a symbol of Indian self-reliance). An entire floor is also devoted to products that come to the rescue of Delhi summer victims, minimising all the damage wrought by sun, dust and heat. For the tender and sunburnt, Khadi's Cucumber Facepack (₹60) is both cooling and restores the glow that sunburn tends to obliterate. Another excellent cooling remedy is the Khadi Mint Soap (₹45), which also comes in khus and aloe vera – all three of which are

naturally soothing ingredients.
Rest your legs in the cafetaria
upstairs when you're done
following Gandhi's footsteps.
*24 Regal Building, Connaught
Place (2336-2231).* ⊖ *Rajiv
Chowk. Daily 10.30am-12.15pm,
1-6.45pm.* ⑰

Mahatta & Co

Mahatta & Co have been in Delhi
since 1947, which makes them one
of India's oldest names in the
business of photography and
printing. They've captured Delhi
from the sepia-tinted days of
buggies and the one-odd car
around Connaught Place to the
modern cornucopia of noise,
colours, vehicles and vitality it
is now. Mahatta's two stores –
the main one in CP and newer
branch in Vasant Kunj, display a
collection of antique photographic equipment, some of which
dates back to 1920, and all of
which is in working condition.

*M-59 Connaught Place (2341-
1962).* ⊖ *Rajiv Chowk. Daily
10.30am-8pm* ⑤⑧

Oxford Book Store

This massive space (4,500 sq ft
of it) is not just limited to books,
DVDs, CDs, and greeting cards.
It also has a Cha Bar that brews
a selection of international teas
and offers munchies from the
kitchens of The Park Hotel. The
selection of books is large, but not
especially inspired, though
Oxford does win the distinction
of Delhi's first shelf dedicated to
alternative sexuality.
*Statesman House, First Floor,
148 Barakhamba Road,
Connaught Place, Outer Circle.
(2376-6080).* ⊖ *Barakhamba
Road. Mon-Sat 10am-9pm,
Sundays noon-9pm.* ⑤⑨

People Tree

This little store, opened in 1990
by a small team of designers,

Khadi Gram Udyog

Janpath

has adamantly held on to its corner in Connaught Place – and its social niche in Delhi. The wares keep changing, as do the social messages on the T-shirts, and the range of accessories has grown from button earrings to lovely glass beads and delicate pin dragonflies. The shop has shelves of traditional "backpacker" material – flowy cotton pants (₹2,700), kurtas (₹400) and tees with popular Indian culture motifs (₹375), as well as hippie bags (₹700-2,000) – each stamped with that oh-so-elusive quality: actual originality. In keeping with the alternative theme, the bookshop tucked away at the back specialises not just in books on Indian cinema, organic farming and environmental politics, it also stocks journals and videotapes that most other bookshops will barely have heard of.
8 Regal Building, Parliament Street (2374-4877). ✪ Rajiv Chowk. Mon-Sat 10am-7pm. ㉚

Around CP

Janpath
Pavement shopping at its best! One of the main arterial roads out of Connaught Place, Janpath has an abundance of stalls selling shoes, jewelery, incense, bags and bric-a-brac, as well as walking vendors selling trinkets, drums, and postcards, particularly to visitors to the city. Expect some hassle. Remember to bargain.
Radial Road 1, Connaught Place, Outer Circle. ✪ Rajiv Chowk. Daily 11am-7pm. ㉛

Palika Bazaar
This underground mega-bazar is either a dream (if you like pirated DVDs) or a nightmare (if you suffer from claustrophobia), but either way it's a fairly amazing glimpse into the future of markets in the year 2091, when there's too many people and no sky.
Connaught Place, Inner Circle. ✪ Rajiv Chowk. Monday to Saturday 11am-8pm. ㉜

Janpath

DELHI BY AREA

Paharganj

For people who avoid psychotropic drugs, a visit to the Paharganj Market is probably the closest thing to getting high (people who don't avoid them have probably already been). The main market, where people of many races, hikers and Hare Krishnas, walk side by side, is a consumerist peace-march, a slice of the kumbh mela-to-Goa scene in the heart of New Delhi.

A multilingual babble fills the speech bubbles that float over the market, where anything can be bought at half-price. Beaded jewellery and shoes, in bright neon and metallic hues, share space with belly dancer outfits. Most stores sell bric-a-brac, "antiques" and the market's most popular item, bongs and bubble pipes in the wildest colours and patterns. Pick up a lipstick bong or even a keychain pipe (for under ₹100), and kinkier types will have a field day with the anatomically-inspired naughty bong (₹250).

In between there are islands of peace in shops like the Jacksons bookshop, which sells titles in nearly a dozen international languages. Ancient traders like the Shringar Hut still persist, braving the explosion of colours

Paharganj

Palika Bazaar

DELHI BY AREA

Jackson Books

One proviso,: you won't find anything with an "Om" on the shoe. Prices run between ₹125 to ₹2,000, depending on the design, but they promise only genuine leather.

Jacksons Books
5106 Main Bazar (5535-1083). Daily 10am-11pm. ⑬

Smoking pipes
Palace Overseas 1570, Main Bazar (2653-4724) ⑭

Aroma Oils
Rama Art Gallery 1550-A Main Bazar (23561836). Daily 10am-8pm. ⑮

Stick-on tattoos
Utsav Bindi Shop 5064/1, Main Bazar (2358-9661). Daily10am-9pm. ⑯

Belly dancer gear
Shahgoofta fashions, 1604, Main Bazar (2358-4764). Daily 10am-10pm. ⑰

Vishal Foot Wear
5082-83, Main Bazar, Paharganj (2358-1960). Daily 11am-8pm. ⑱

and sound and still selling cold-pressed sweet almond oil extracted with a desi kohlu (stone mill). Also check out Vishal Foot Wear, a shop with almost every square inch of its walls covered in shoes ranging from colourful flip-flops to curly-toed kohlapuris.

24/7

Agni

Nightlife

24/7

A bar that's really truly open around the clock is an exciting proposition in Delhi. The interior of 24/7 is stylishly masculine, with a lot of leather – from the comfy sofa-chairs to the barstools – as well as wood, granite and marble. The bar counter itself is lit from within, a nice little touch that transmits itself to the rest of the surroundings. 24/7 has a wine cellar attached, and has a pretty good wine list, with wineries from France, Australia, California, New Zealand, Italy and South America well-represented. Many are available by the glass, priced in the region of ₹400 upward.
The Lalit, *Barakhamba Road, Connaught Place (4444-7777). ⊖ Barakhamba Road. Daily 24 hours. Night out for two ₹2,500.*⊕

Agni

Sashay through the love-bead curtains and find yourself in a dark, compact bar festooned with radiant highlights – and Connaught Place's most

consistently happening dance-floor. Designed by London's Conran and Partners, Agni channels a '60s mod mood and an underground vibe, with bar staff in Rohit Bal outfits and a highly creative cocktail menu. There are plenty of cosy nooks filled with leather sofas and bean-bags. Agni pulls in the Punjabi boyz, wannabe-models and expats every night of the week, and is especially packed on Friday and Saturday nights. The dance floor is small, but there is room enough to dance and not just bop – just watch out for those flailing elbows when the bhangra starts to beat.
The Park, *15 Parliament Street, Connaught Place (2374-3000) Daily 11am-1am. Night out for two ₹3,500.* ⑩

Aura

The vodka bar at the Claridges, is always fairly busy, with hotel residents and a stream of smartly suited professionals milling about. The décor is self-consciously cosmopolitan and, really, indistinguishable from any other

Lap

lounge-bar. The impressive vodka menu features more brands than you can shake a stick at: from the obscure to the more commonplace; from Poland, France, Finland, UK, Sweden, Russia and the USA. Be adventurous and pass on the Absolut and Grey Gooses. Consider instead the wasabi breakfast-ini or the spicelandic, made with coriander-infused vodka. A shot of vodka clocks in anywhere between ₹250 and ₹375. There's a great selection of beer, from Foster's to Asahi (ranging from ₹240 to ₹390), and the food menu offers up everything from bar snacks to Asian bowl food. *The Claridges*, *12 Aurangzeb Road (4133-5133). Daily 4pm-1am. Night out for two* ₹ *3,000.* ⑪

Lap

Lap was Delhi's first members'-only nightclub – to get in, you must be a member or on a member's list. But these rules are only for the main club, which is indoors and accessible from the lobby. The beautiful garden restaurant and outdoor bar are open to the public every night. There's a baroque fountain in the centre with a broad, perch-friendly parapet running around it as clusters of sunken and elevated table settings contend with each other. The average cost of a cocktail is ₹400, which means the place promises a great party and no one has to feel uninvited. *Hotel Samrat*, *Chanakyapuri (2410-3762). Mon-Sat 12.30pm-12.30am. Night out for two* ₹ *4,000.* ⑫

Rick's

At Rick's, you'll find a succinct selection of molecular cocktails in the "atomic" section. Ask nicely, and award-winning bartender Anup Negi will whip up a martini foam or some whiskey sour caviar for you. Rick's serves different versions – whiskey sour caviar and blueberry martini caviar

Lap

DELHI's AWARD WINNING NIGHTCLUB

In the Lap of Luxury
Hello

The Garden of Gastronomy
Mail Today

Champagne dipped nights amidst amber faceted
crystal and velvet gift wrapped memorable experiences
Harpers Bazaar

Weekends in Delhi will never be the same again
Indian Express

w Delhi 21   or Reservations +

Saqi

among them. These are made by combining the liqueur with sodium alginate and calcium chloride in a complex process that can take hours. You can have them either as part of your drink, heaped at the bottom of the corresponding cocktail, or separately. Get the deconstructed version, a heap of green pearls laid out on a soup spoon, with a shot of crème de menthe to accompany them. Rick's, incidentally, also serves the tallest glass of beer in Delhi (650ml, ₹420-695 depending on the beer).
***Taj Mahal Hotel**, 1 Mansingh Road (2302-6162). Mon-Fri 12.30pm-1am, Sat & Sun 12.30pm-3am. Night out for two ₹4,500.* ⑬

Saqi

With mirror-lined corridors and red lights turning in cages, Saqi – better known as just Alka, after the 40-year old hotel it's located in – was always as woozy and lurid as only the '70s could be. After an ill-judged renovation in 2008,

much of that was lost, but much remains. The glittery, high-backed bar chairs are still cinematic, other patrons still look mysterious, and the ambience persists. There's a cozy smokers' terrace, and its true the place feels more women-friendly than it used to.
***Hotel Alka**, 16/90 P-Block Connaught Circus (2334-4000). ⊖ Rajiv Chowk. Daily 11am-11pm. Happy hours 11am-7pm. Night out for two ₹1,000.* ㉔

Cinemas

One of the best things about three-hour-long Bollywood releases in the summer is that you can dash off to air-conditioned cinemas. Delhi got its first AC cinema in 1954, and though both the now beautifully refurbished Delite and the classic Golcha vie for credit, Delite appears to have won the case.
Delite *4/1 Delite Cinema Building, Asaf Ali Road.* **Enquiry** *2327-2549.* **Ticket** *₹25-130.* **Credit Card** *No*

Odeon *D- Block, Inner Circle, Connaught Place.* ⊖ *Rajiv Chowk* **Enquiry** *2341-2217, 4151-7899* **Tickets** *₹50-80* **Credit Card** *Yes* **Facilities** *Snack bar, wheelchair access.*

PVR Plaza *H-Block, Connaught Place.* ⊖ *Rajiv Chowk* **Enquiry** *4166-3787* **Advance Booking** *4166-3787* **Tickets** *₹125-160* **Credit Card** *Yes* **Facilities** *Snack bar, wheelchair access, home delivery facilities at extra charges.*

Live Music

The Attic
This little spot has shaped its attic-ness into a fine small theatre where you might find a recitation of Urdu dastans (epic tales), a "food meditation" workshop or a queer performance night. *36 Regal Building, Connaught Place (2374-6050).* ⊖ *Rajiv Chowk. Visit www.theatticdelhi.org..* ⑮

@live
An exception to the usual rule of dining in Delhi, where live music comes second to the chatter of oblivious patrons. @live is intimate and stylish, reminiscent (we'd like to think) of someplace in downtown New York. Red brick walls have gold accents, and mellow lighting focuses on the house band led by Francis Anthony Rozells. Even though they play covers, their real selling-point is their own acoustic interpretations. There's even a song menu along with the standard food menu with over 450 songs. Greater emphasis has been placed in the appetisers rather than the main course, so snack on their excellent cheesy mozzarella fingers or the apricot-glazed lamb satay with peanut sauce. *K-12, Connaught Place, Outer Circle (4356-0008).* ⊖*Rajiv Chowk. Daily noon-midnight. Visa and Mastercard accepted. Meal for two ₹2,500.* ⑱

@live

DELHI BY AREA

Arts & Leisure

Amatrra spa

One of Delhi's favourite spas, Amattra has been around for a while but constantly updates its ayurvedically inspired menu of treatments and massages (from ₹3000).

The Ashok, 50-B Chanakyapuri (2412-2921). Daily 9am-10pm; Le Meridien Hotel, 8 Windsor Place, Janpath (2371-0101). Daily 7.15am-10pm.

arts.i

Quickly establishing its relevance to the city's arts, this modern, spacious gallery has an attached café and giftshop worthy of some distracted browsing. Notable for staying open late.

7 Atmaram Mansion, Level One, Scindia House, Kasturba Gandhi Marg (4372-7000). ☉ Rajiv Chowk. Daily 10am-11pm.

The India Habitat Centre and Visual Arts Gallery

The India Habitat Centre is a cultural hub of auditoria and nice spaces, which is perenially busy during the good weather. The Visual Arts Gallery, curated by Alka Pande, has been at the centre of much attention, with several distinguished artists and sculptors displayed here.

Lodhi Road, near Sai Baba Mandir. (2436-6204) Monday to Saturday 10am-8pm.

India International Centre

The intellectual hearth of New Delhi, and probably the country, hosts all manner of cultural events and discussions. Unfortunately the cafeteria and restaurant are for members only.

40, Max Mueller Marg, Lodhi Estate (24619431).

Indira Gandhi National Centre for the Arts

Twenty years after the Centre was inaugurated, its construction is still in progress. Yet since early 2010, the white elephant has shown signs of changing its colours, hosting a stream

The India Habitat Centre

India International Centre

of lovely and uncommon performing-arts events.
1 CV Mess, Janpath, near Le Meridien (2338-9675). ㉞

Kamani Auditorium
One of the largest, oldest and most prominent auditoria in Delhi, Kamani has excellent facilities including a stage with an orchestra pit. The auditorium hosts plays, concerts, ballets and other dance performances, and the best international troupes visiting the capital.
1 Copernicus Marg (2338-8084, 4350-3351) ⊖ Mandi House. ㉜

The National Gallery of Modern Art
The National Gallery of Modern Art was set up in 1954 to house visual and sculptural works from the 1850s onwards. Though the

National Gallery of Modern Art

The travel apps city lovers have been waiting for…

Apps and maps work offline with no roaming charges

Search for 'Time Out Guides' in the app store

timeout.com/iphonecityguides

Kamani Auditorium

permanent collection isn't well-organised and big shows are few and far between, there's no denying that the NGMA houses some of the finest work by Indian and international artists. Some of the best works that remain on display are Amrita Sher-Gil's portraits and some drawings and paintings by Tagore. In 2009, a new wing was added, adding almost six times the space to the existing gallery. There's also a cafeteria and museum shop selling cheap, quality prints of canonical modern Indian paintings.
Jaipur House, India Gate (2338-6111). Tue-Sun 10am-5pm. Closed on all national holidays. Indians ₹10, others ₹150, students & children ₹1. ㉝

Palette Art Gallery
Curated by the fashion designer pair Rohit Gandhi and Rahul Khanna, Palette allegedly sells close to 90 per cent of its art within a fortnight of an exhibition. Opening nights allow you to rub bare shoulders with New Delhi's swish set.
14 Golf Links, second floor (4174-3034). Daily 11am-7pm ㉞

Triveni Kala Sangam
There are four galleries in this complex. One is located in the basement and is run by the Art Heritage group. Then there is the Sridharani gallery that holds regular shows by both established and young artists, while the Triveni Gallery displays more experimental work. The centre also has a Scultpure Court, and a well-stocked bookshop that has an unconventional index of books, journals and cassettes. Done quibbling over the art? Have a nibble at the Triveni Tea Terrace (p105).
205 Tansen Marg (2371-8833). Ⓔ Mandi House. Mon-Sat 10am-7pm. ㉟

Shri Ram Centre
The Shri Ram Centre for performing arts is one of the flagship theatres of Mandi House, Delhi's undisputed theatre district (also see Kamani Theatre in this section). It's a well-equipped auditorium, where most of Delhi's celebrated Hindi-language plays are performed, with an attached canteen, bookshop and library.
4 Safdar Hashmi Marg (2371-4307). Ⓔ Mandi House. ㊱

DELHI BY AREA

South West

The Qutab Minar

Dilli Haat

THE OLDEST & THE NEWEST

Unlike any other sector of the city, south Delhi contains an amazing combination of historical monuments and modern cosmopolitan life: it's where Delhi's best restaurants, bars and shopping are located. In fact, the phrase "south Delhi" is synonymous with the comfortable life (or the pampered life, if you're from elsewhere).

We're calling "southwest Delhi" everything west of the busy Bus Rapid Transport Corridor, which bisects south Delhi. It's a serendipitous description: the spine that runs down southwest Delhi is Aurobindo Marg, which follows the exact course used by the Mughals and the British to get from Old Delhi (or sixteenth-century Shahjahanabad, in the north) and the oldest Delhi (or the eleventh- to fifteenth-century cities of Mehrauli, Siri and Jahanpanah in the southwest). The area's crowning jewel is the Qutab Minar, marking the southern-most extent of Delhi's past city walls.

After the ancient cities were vacated, the area reverted to an open mix of marsh, fields and revered tombs and graveyards. Today, of course, it is choc-a-bloc with high-rent residential enclaves, and markets that range from streetside bargains (Sarojini Nagar) to cute boutique fashion (Hauz Khas Village) and popular mega-malls (Saket). Whether it's shopping, clubbing or just a lungful of oxygen in a neighbourhood park, you'll be spoilt for choice. But southwest Delhi's greatest pleasure is wandering through a modern neighbourhood and stumbling on a forgotten mosque, a prayer wall, or a tomb that's hundreds of years old.

SELECT
CITYWALK
Go Shopping!

Saket, New Delhi

The Widest in Choices, The Best in Brands.

Housing some of the most exciting Indian & International brands under one roof, Select CITYWALK invites you to come experience a vibrant, upscale, one of a kind shopping and leisure environment in the heart of South Delhi. The combination of Luxury and High Street shopping, with a midweek Flea Market on Wednesday, 6 Screen PVR Cinemas & Family Entertainment Centre "Hangout" will certainly have you asking for more.

So what are you waiting for?

get haute
at Select CITYWALK

Sights & Museums

Begampur Masjid

As an island of piety and community in the middle of the madness of the Old City, Jama Masjid's impact is unbeatable. But if you're curious about the *masjid-i-jamis* that preceded Shahjahan's glorious one, a wonderful surprise awaits you in the Begumpur Masjid. Venture through the urban villages of Begumpur and Kalu Sarai, and locate the heart of the fourteenth-century Tughlaq city of Jahanpanah (the fourth of the seven cities of ancient Delhi). This massive stone mosque may be bare of ornamentation – characteristic of the Tughlaq era – but it is magnificent. Search for staircases that lead all the way to the roof of the main portal. It has fallen far outside the tourist circuit, and the locals seem to have forgotten about it, which makes the sense of antiquity even more powerful. Even on a pleasant day, you'll only have a couple of kite flyers for company. *Five-minute walk from Sarvapriya Vihar. ⊖ Hauz Khas. Open sunrise-sunset. Entry free.* ❶

Begampur Masjid

Garden of Five Senses

DELHI BY AREA

Garden of Five Senses

Amidst the concrete jungle of the city, the Garden of Five Senses does a good job of stimulating all five senses. From the ethereal wind-chime tree to the sculpted elephant waterfalls, well-tended flower beds, and gorgeously located restaurants and bars (Magique, Fio and The Zoo), there are few places in any Indian city quite like it. Regular art shows and concerts also take place. *Westend Marg, Said-ul-Ajaib, off Mehrauli-Badarpur Road. (2653-4401, 2651-0519). Daily 6am-9pm. Entry ₹15 per person.* ❷

Hauz Khas madrassa

A placid lake created in the thirteenth century by Alauddin Khilji, fringed by a handsome madrassa built in the fourteenth-century by Firoz Shah Tughlaq, surrounded by a trendy little conglomeration of arts boutiques and restaurants which is very twenty-first century (see Hauz Khas Village on p146). There are

Mehrauli Archaeological Park

two separate entrances – one leads down to a walkway around the lake, another to the madrassa high on the embankment. The balconies over the lake are a great fplace to unwind with a picnic. *Through Hauz Khas Village, behind Green Park Market.* ⊖ *Green Park. Open sunrise-sunset. Entry free.* ❸

Qutab Minar + Mehrauli Archaeological Park

When it was constructed in 1192, and for a good while after, the Qutab Minar was the tallest man-made structure in the world. It was built by Qutab-ud-din Aibak, the founder of the Slave Dynasty, and his successors added to the mosques and tombs of the monumental park around it. Look out for the iron pillar nearby, which has stood for 1,600 years without any rusting, a sign of ancient metallurgical skill. By legend, if you can stand with your back to the pillar and still touch your fingers (after wrapping your arms around it behind you), any wish you make will be granted. The pillar is fenced off now, and

entry into the Qutab Minar has been restricted since a stampede thirty years ago killed 45 people, including several school children. But the World Heritage Site is unmissable. Other impressive structures in the complex are the Alai Darwaza (Alai Gate) and the Quwwat-ul-Islam Mosque.

Leave time to wander through the park that spreads for 100 acres around the complex. This area was once the favourite hunting site for Mughal princes and later a weekend retreat for British colonial officials. The park's monuments include Balban's tomb, in which Qutb's successor is buried; the three-storeyed Rajon Ki Baoli stepwell and the five-storeyed sulphur-smelling Gandhak Ki Baoli step well. Check out Jamali Kamali, the shared tomb of a Sufi poet and his alleged male lover. If nothing else, you'll learn how to compress a millennium of built history into one afternoon. For a guided walk, contact the Indian National Trust for Art and Cultural Heritage (2464-1304). *Aurobindo Marg, 15km south of Connaught Place.* ↔ *Qutab Minar. Daily sunrise-sunset. Entry* ₹10

Indians; ₹ *250 others.* ❹

STADIA Jawaharlal Nehru Stadium
You're unlikely to miss the winged roof of Delhi's flagship stadium, even if you aren't catching any events here. It hosts the opening and closing ceremonies, track & field events and marathon. *Pragati Vihar, Lodhi Colony.* ↔ *JLN Stadium, Jor Bagh* ❺
RK Khanna Tennis Complex
Tennis. ↔ *Green Park* ❻
Siri Fort Sports Complex
Badminton, squash. ↔ *Green Park* ❼
Thyagaraj Sports Complex
Netball. ↔*INA Market* ❽

Eating & Drinking

Blue Bar
One of Delhi's rare genuine lounge bars. A single irridescent room, glowing in spots of valentine red and marine blues and purples, is warmed by the golden light of chandeliers. The drinks menu is innovative and delightful: try the coffee-and-passionfruit margarita (₹650), a blend of Patron tequila, Grand

DELHI BY AREA

Home & Lifestyle

SELECT **CITYWALK** Go Shopping! Saket, New Delhi

Episode | Goodearth | Homestop | Maspar | Oma | Rosebys | U |

www.selectcitywalk.com

South West

Mariner and Kahlua shaken with passionfruit and lime juice. *The Taj Palace Hotel, Sardar Patel Marg, Diplomatic Enclave (2611-0202). Sun-Thur 12.30pm-12.30am; Fri-Sat 12.30pm-2am. Meal for two ₹3,000.* ⑨

Dilli Haat

You're in Delhi, but you want to get a taste of Kerala's kappa and meen curry (fish curry and tapioca), Maharasthra's sabudana vada (sago-pearl fritters), and Manipur's oksa angoba (pork curry)? The only place to go is Dilli Haat, where nearly every Indian state has a food-stall, and most of them are surprisingly good quality. Vegetarians should sound out the special thali at the Rajasthan stall. The Chungudi nadia rasa, a dish consisting of large prawns simmered in coconut milk is finger-licking fantastic at the Orissa stall. Thrill-seekers should look out for dishes at the Nagaland stall prepared with raja mircha, officially the hottest chilli in the world. Also see Shopping in this chapter.
Opposite INA market. ⊖ *INA Market. Daily 11am-10pm. No alcohol. Meal for two ₹260.* ⑩

Blue Bar

Gunpowder

Gunpowder

When owner-chef Satish Warier opened Gunpowder, lovers of Malayali food discovered an unreal view of the Hauz Khas reservoir as well as magically soft, flaky porottas. Since then, no restaurant in Delhi has been more talked about than this tiny, laid-back eyrie over the lake. Try the mutton koothu porotta, a rich jumble of juicy meat, bread and spices and a perfect meal for one. Alternatively, a few plates of Coorg pandicurry, tangy toddyshop meen curry and avial will leave a whole table happy.

22 Hauz Khas Village, third floor (2653-5700). Daily noon-4pm, 7-11pm. Meal for two ₹800. ⑪

Izakaya

A sake bar that encourages its customers to enjoy both the sake and the shochu-inflected cocktails even if patrons have to slur their final orders.

***DLF Promenade Mall** 317, Nelson Mandela Marg, Vasant Kunj (4665-6317). Daily noon-3.30pm; 6.30-11.30pm. All credit*

DELHI BY AREA

Izakaya

cards except Diner's Club. Meal for two ₹4,000. ⑫

Kainoosh

Try out the 'bespoke' thali, which involves a solemn procession of dishes to the table and features the exquisite lamb flavoured with roasted almond paste, tasting emphatically of good lamb, and not weighed down by its complicated dressing. Small prawns in cinnamon-tomato gravy are rich and satisfying and raita with crispy ladies' finger slivers is a welcome diversion from all the

meat. The menu may overturn things you thought you knew – about portions, flavours, combinations – but give yourself over to the capable kitchens. *DLF Promenade Mall, ground floor, Nelson Mandela Marg, Vasant Kunj (95607-15544). Daily 12:30pm-3:30pm; 7:30pm-1am. Alcohol served. All credit cards accepted. Meal for two ₹2,400.* ⑬

Magique

It's not hyperbole to say this is one of the most beautiful spots

Kainoosh

in town. The restaurant, with its glass façade and fantastic prints, is surrounded by a candle-and-lantern-lit paradise. Think frangipani trees, pebbled walks and wrought-iron light fixtures. All martinis are a flat ₹475 but try the golden martini (which features champagne and the elderflower herb). Try the starter plates of warm plenta cakes with truffle oil (₹375) and batter prawns with chilli and Thai basil sauce (₹525). *The Garden Village, Gate No 3, Garden of Five Senses, Said-ul-Ajaib (3271-6767). Daily 7.30pm-* *1am. Meal for two ₹2,500.* ⑬

Naivedyam

Turn into Hauz Khas Village for the splendidly overwrought south Indian atmoshphere of Naivedyam. A Nandi graces the entrance to the cool, dark restaurant (good in the summer) and a hot glass of rasam graces your palate before a meal (good in the winter). The walls are heavy with Tanjore murals, the cooks are from Madurai – you could nickname it Tamil By Nature, even though the owner is from

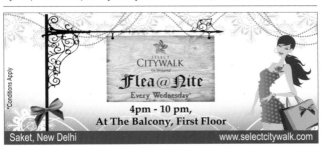

Magique

Mangalore.
1Hauz Khas Village, (2653-6045).
Daily 11am-11pm. All major
credit cards accepted. Meal for
two ₹400. ⑮

Nanking

The best thing on Baba Ling's
restaurant, which put Vasant
Kunj on the food map a few years
ago, has to be the crab (from
₹1,400 onward). The crabs are
"alive, alive oh" before they're
cooked, and the price depends on
the size of the crustacean. The
flavours of the black bean sauce
are beautifully balanced, and
collectively complement the
natural taste of the crab itself. It
looks good too. Slip on your bib
and get cracking, and never mind
who you splatter. There's also a
gloriously decadent buffet with
some 18-odd varieties of dim sum.
If your stomach isn't crying out
for mercy at the end, finish up
with sesame honey noodles and
vanilla ice cream.

Nanking

Plot C-6, Vasant Kunj, opposite Delhi Public School (2613-8936) Sat and Sun, 12.30-4pm. Weekend dim sum buffet ₹850 + tax. Includes one 650ml bottle of Tiger beer. ⑯

My Humble House
A hip rooftop Chinese restaurant at the Maurya, expect foie gras and the like with a spectacular wine menu. No, not Punjabi-Chinese. The outside seating accommodates 16 covers; if you have a big party, they'll seat the lot. Expensive, but fantastic views across the Ridge, and a little pool below your feet. Bring a shawl.
ITC Maurya Hotel Sardar Patel Marg, Diplomatic Enclave (2611-2233). Daily 7pm-12.30am. Meal for two ₹6,000. ⑰

Punjabi by Nature
Punjabi by Nature is most famous for pioneering the vodka golguppa – an innocuous sweet-

DELHI BY AREA

Punjabi by Nature

sour street snack turned cocktail conversation piece. That's only the first example of how truly this restaurant lives up to its name. Large stone walls with water shimmering down them, a fountain out front and grand tables with majestic silver chalices for water set the tone. Besides the vodka golguppas, get the dal makhani and the raan-e-Punjab. The tandoori jhinga is our pick of the clay oven, but you would do well ordering the

chicken or burra kababs. Round this off with gulab jamuns flambéd in brandy.
11 Basant Lok, Vasant Vihar (4151-6666). Daily 12.30-11pm. Meal for two ₹2,500. ⑱

Rosang's
There's no place like Rosang's. Run by Manipuri sisters Mary Tongsung and Mamaan Khuplong, this tiny shop sells specialities from India's North-eastern states, like the Khasi kwai (betel nut and paan leaf), dried fish and mushrooms, and fresh bamboo shoot. At the attached restaurant, couple Lalmuan Ching and Kham Lalmuan serve mostly Manipuri and Mizo dishes, although Ching is happy to whip up some Naga food too. The speciality is her Naga-style pork curry with bamboo shoot. And they also have the elusive axone, a Naga preparation of soybean cooked and dried, and then fermented in banana leaves.
1385A/5 Rama Market, basement, Munirka, opposite MCD Park (98118-98923). Daily 10am-10pm. No alcohol served. No credit cards. Meal for two ₹150. ⑲

The capital and the beach

In 2007, Olive brought the beach to Delhi. And with it, all things Olive: a Mediterranean air, infectious bonhomie and cuisine like none other.

At Olive Beach, Chef Saby introduces the good people of Delhi to Europe's best loved culinary creations. Come over to the capital's very own beach and discover why it's so favoured by every gourmet worth his salt.

Olive Beach Delhi has been chosen Premium Restaurant Brand of the Year at the Golden Spoon Awards 2009; and one of Delhi, NCR's Finest Restaurants at Mail Today's Best of the Best Awards, 2010.

OLIVE BEACH

Olive Beach, Hotel Diplomat, 9 Sardar Patel Marg, Diplomatic Enclave, Chanakya Puri, New Delhi - 21.
Tel.: (011) 46040404 / 99711 44455. www.olivebarandkitchen.com. Join the Olive Beach, Delhi group on Facebook.

Rosang's

Sartoria

Pair some fine Italian food with wine and live music at Sartoria. Ask for their special promotions; they usually have a specially designed four-course meal on Fridays, which is laid out with choice international wines.

Smokehouse Deli

18-A, Basant Lok, Priya Cinema Complex, Vasant Vihar (98711-54499). Timings Noon-11pm. Meal for two ₹3,000. ㉚

Smokehouse Deli

The décor at this young sibling of the Smokehouse Grill (p175) is refreshingly simple: creamy white with black line drawings, quirky lamps and an odd collection of books. This distnctly un-mall-like theme continues onto a sunny deck with a white picket fence in the central courtyard of the DLF Place mall. It's perfect when you're sampling the Deli's breakfast offerings (pancakes, cereals, bagels, eggs, bacon and sausages), or lingering over their wasabi and saffron pappardelle with a glass of Belgian beer. DLF Place, ground floor, Nelson Mandela Marg, Vasant Kunj (4607-5646). Daily breakfast 10am-noon, lunch noon-3.30pm, all day menu 3.30pm-7.30pm, *dinner 7.30pm-midnight. Meal for two ₹2,700.* ㉑

Swagath

A family-style restaurant with powerful air-conditioning and ice cold beer, specialising in fiery hot south Indian seafood dishes. Swagath features Mangalore, Malabar and Chettinad coastal cuisines. Try the prawns butter garlic or fish gassi. The north Indian "Mughlai" food isn't too bad (we like the tandoori prawns), but please, avoid the Chinese.
14 Defence Colony Market (2433-7538). Daily 11am-11.45pm. Meal for two ₹1,500. ㉒

Tamura

The closest thing Delhi has to a neighbourhood Japanese restaurant serves a range of home-style fare, mostly to expats. Settle into tatami-and-rice-paper booths and sip sake while you're choosing from cooked sushi (tempura rolls, California rolls, etc), raw sushi and sashimi (available fresh, only on Fridays and Saturdays), teriyaki fish and other, more exotic, items.
8 D Block Market, Poorvi Marg, Vasant Vihar (2615-4082). Daily noon-3pm; 6.30pm-10:30pm. Meal for two ₹1,200. ㉓

Tapas

Rumour had it that Tapas at the Jaypee Vasant Continental had a chicken tikka sushi roll. We went to investigate and found that they do have an array of Indian fusion sushi – like the seekh kabab sushi – but don't worry, the chicken is cooked. Chef Vijay presents these Japanese-style, with wasabi, pickled ginger, soy sauce, and an additional bowl of green chutney. It works surprisingly well. Chicken tikka plus wasabi? Who would have thought it?
***Jaypee Vasant Continental**, New Delhi, Vasant Vihar (4600-*

DELHI BY AREA

Zaffarani Zaika

South West

8800). Daily 11am-12.45am. Meal for two ₹1,500 @

Zaffarani Zaika

There's a crisp, focused menu: two pages of kababs, a page of curries and a biryani special. The vegetarian starters sound yummy, but we insist you try the Shahjahani Shikhampur kababs and the seekh-boti kababs, as well as some of their mains: the Beli Ram ka gosht, the nihari Awadhi biryani, and the murg massallam. Zaffarani Zaika's menu doesn't do ritzy spins on dozens of cuisines, but instead focuses on more local crowd-pleasers like murgh parcha kabab and ulte tawe ki roti. It's all in the little details – the frosty glasses, cold face towels, the chutneys, the minty seasoning and the complexity in the kababs. *Yashwant Place near Bikanerwala, Chanakyapuri (97171-76552). Daily noon-midnight. Meal for two ₹2,000.* @

Dilli Haat

Dilli Haat is one of those rare, inspired experiments with public space that brings together rural artisans, middle-class families, young Delhi hipsters and visiting tourists. Created in 1994 in an attempt to recreate the feel of a village market, this unique open-air bazaar is one of Delhi's most popular shopping venues for handloom and handicraft items. The 200 (or thereabouts) permanent stalls are rented out to craftspersons from all over India for 15 days at a time, enabling them direct access to consumers. The complex also has 25 food stalls representing the different states of India. Themed festivals here often includes lively cultural programmes. You'll never leave empty-handed. Also see Eating & drinking in this section. *Sri Aurobindo Marg, opposite INA Market (2611-9055).* ⊖ *INA*

Dilli Haat

Market. Open daily 11am-10pm. Admission: ₹15. 26

Fact and Fiction

The niche and proportionately minute Fact and Fiction, located bang opposite the Priya Cinema in Basant Lok market, offers a selection rather than the collection of books you'd find at bigger stores. You don't get any discounts but it's a charming joint with refined and surprising shelves (especially for fiction), an extremely erudite owner and great music on the speakers.
39 Basant Lok Market, Vasant Vihar (2614-6843). Wed-Mon 11am-8pm. 27

Happily Unmarried

This product design outfit does quirky but very useable lifestyle goods. The "shoes and egos outside" coir mats, the old Indian lavatory-shaped ashtrays, the shotglasses with famous gansters' faces on them – each of their

Fact and Fiction

products has a goofy Indian twist. They're ideal for presents for friends, and not just for the lads. Consider their "man dice" for women. Each roll of the dice produces a romantic outcome: "Mr so hot, but so not right for you", "Mr take home to your Mother" or even, "Mr Right Now".

Happily Unmarried

Hauz Khas Village

5M Shahpur Jat (3254-2988). Mon-Sat 10am-7pm. Visit www.happilyunmarried.com for a complete list of stores. ㉔

Hauz Khas Village

Until quite recently a genuine village (pressed up against the premises of the fourteenth-century Hauz Khas madrassa), Hauz Khas Village has become a cool little pile-up of design boutiques, handicrafts stores, and sui generis bohemian attractions like the Yodakin independent bookshop (p148) and the Kunzum Traveller's Café with good coffee and Wi-fi for free (great for exchanging tips). There's no more attractive shopping locality in town. Take the winding back routes from Aurobindo Market and look out for dealers who specialise in vintage posters (you'll find some Bollywood gems, mainly starring Amitabh Bachchan), lithographs and old maps. To put your feet up with a beer or some dinner there's Gunpowder (p135), or The Living Room Café (p157) for beer and live music. And a whole bunch of little shops worth popping in to.

Kunzum Travellers' Cafe

T-49, ground floor, Hauz Khas Village (2651-3949, 96507-02777). Tues-Sun 11am-7.30pm. ㉙

Hidesign

The sophistication and quality of Hidesign's bags have made it practically the default option for any Dilliwala looking for leather – or for a gift that's handsome and still affordable for a man in your life. Every bag is handmade, and even the brass buckles are individually cast and polished. *No 67, Select CityWalk Mall, first floor, District Centre, Saket (4054-8821); G-18, Ambience Mall, Nelson Mandela Road, Vasant Kunj (4087-0047); S-04, MGF Metropolitan Mall, second floor, Mehrauli-Gurgaon Road, Gurgaon (0124-4019446).* ㉚

O Palacio

It's been a quick trip from social Siberia to cultural Iberia for Hauz Rani, an unfavoured urban village opposite the giant mall-strip of Saket. But O Palacio has brought in a startling touch of Portuguese-inspired luxury. It's a small hub of art, food and fashion enterprises: the Galeria de Art, the Casa Portugesa restaurant, and the studios of four designers – Nakul Sen, Shyam Narayan Prasad, Zoya and Gayatri Khanna. Getting here is a little bit of an adventure, but O Palacio itself is a diamond in

rough surroundings, which makes it all the more attractive.
E-12/70 Hauz Rani, opposite DLF Mall Saket (2667-2896). Tue-Sun 11am-8.30pm. ③

Midland Bookshop
Every book is on discount all year round at this classic bookstore. They have another branch in South Extension with lots of space to sit and browse but we prefer this one for the charmingly cluttered atmosphere.
20 Aurobindo Place, Hauz Khas (2696-2718). Daily 10.30am-8.30pm. ③

Play Clan
The Play Clan is a group of designers selling jazzed up, humorous, affordable souveniers that pretty much nailed the new kitsch aesthetic so adored in Delhi today. Most of their products have an urban-Indian motif woven into them: Their Ambassador car (an Indian icon) series that runs through artwork and tee-shirts is one example. You'll find everything from lamps to notebooks to personalized sneakers here, including a fair amount of graphic art.
G-07C, Select CityWalk Mall, ground floor, District Centre, Saket (4053-4559); daily 11am-9pm. Shop No 14, The Garden Village, East Bazaar, The Garden of Five Senses, Said-ul-Ajaib (3242-8087); Wed-Mon 11.30am-11pm. Visit www.theplayclan.com. ③

Saket mall strip
The most central of Delhi's five mall districts, Saket was transfor-

Midland Bookshop

med when the Select CityWalk, MGF Metropolitan and DLF Place malls erupted out of the earth like a shining mountain-range. CityWalk is the unquestioned titan of Delhi mall culture, hosting art shows, theatre and music in its front courtyard. Also see Hidesign and Play Clan in this section.
District Centre, Saket. ③

Sarojini Nagar
Rumours circulate perpetually in women's colleges in Delhi about what's in the lanes of Sarojini Nagar this month: Mango dresses, ₹150 with only a button missing, satin shoes, sequined linen harem pants and the legendary "ten-rupee pile", which harbours incredible bargains as well as embarrassing duds. The street bazaar is nobody's secret, and probably wields more influence on fashion in south Delhi than all its designer boutiques put together.

DELHI BY AREA

South West

But Sarojini Nagar is also a household market that sells vegetables, linen and kitchenware. *11am-9pm. Partially closed on Mondays.* ⑯

Shahpur Jat

An urban village settlement dating back 900 years, the galis of Shahpur Jat are teeming with little designer ateliers and custom couture studios. It's less a market than a congregation of young creatives sporting spools of fabric and the odd latte from The Coffee Garage. But it's the buzzy new spots that pop up (and disappear with equal regularity) that make it worth a regular wander – you'll find shoes, clothes, quilts, trunks, and wonderful bric-a-brac.

Alter Ego *87 B Shahpur Jat (4175-1846).* ⑯

The MaxiMum Store *5-J/1, ground floor (4616-8026).* ㊲

Santina *113-A/1, Shahpur Jat (2649-7174).* ⑱

The Shoe Garage *118-B, next to*

Shahpur Jat

SBI (2649-8404). ㊴

Yodakin

Tucked into the labyrinthine by-lanes of Hauz Khas Village sits Yodakin, a welcoming little cupboard of a bookshop with a focus on independent publishers. Left Word, Blaft, Palador, Women

Sarojini Nagar

Unlimited, Seagull Books and Yoda Press rub worthy shoulders on its shelves. A slim ladder leads to a mezzanine, with more books. Delhi's independent publishing houses field great reviews and talented authors, but retail stores are squeamish about stocking their titles. Niche producers are raising the bar for Indian media publishing, striking out in brave and weird directions. Yodakin brings those efforts together in one place, from Underscore music titles to the Under Construction documentary collection.
2 Hauz Khas Village (2653-6283). Visit www.yodakin.com. Wed-Mon 10.30am-7.30pm, Tue 2-7.30pm. ⁴⁹

Nightlife

Ikko Lounge

Ikko Lounge can be nice when you want to have a quiet night with friends (this applies solely to weekdays). With large, comfy velvet sofas that are ideal for sinking into and burgundy-flushed mood lighting, this place is perfect for a never-ending heart-to-heart with your best friend.
***Lazeez Affaire Complex**, Malcha Marg Shopping Centre, Chanakyapuri. (2687-8155) Daily Noon-1am. Night out for two ₹3,000* ⁴¹

ai

ai's Japanese aesthetic is glamorous and dramatic and the adjacent terrace with loungey alcoves and long, covered tables is entrancing in good weather. As much a showcase for its fresh Tsukiji-sourced seafood as for the pretty, wealthy people who lap it up, The Love Hotel is also a choice venue for music gigs. The tall cocktail glasses with zig-zag stems fit the settings. The Hayato Brothers cocktail, the perky gin fizz and the peach martini are good ways to start the night, and the rest of the cocktail list will keep you going till morning.
MGF Metropolitan Mall, second

Yodakin

South West

floor, District Centre, Saket (4065-4567). All major cards accepted. Daily 12.30-3.30pm; 7-11.45pm. Night out for two ₹4,000+. ⊙

Café Morrison

Named after the late frontman of The Doors, this café shuns any music apart from rock 'n' roll and (closely) related genres. Since it opened in 2005, Café Morrison has held weekly live gigs on Sunday nights, which are hugely popular with the black T-shirt brigade (call the venue, or pick up *Time Out*, to confirm a gig). They also host classic rock Retro nights once a month and resident DJ Maddy plays rock tunes every night. The crowd is mostly the college-going lot, though you'll also find the occasional 50-year-old. Upstairs is where Bass Foundation let rip some drum 'n' bass every odd Tuesday as well. *E 12, 1st and 2nd floor, South Extension II (6510-6169). Daily 11am-11.30pm. Night out for two ₹1,500.* ⊙

Golden Dragon

You know you've reached the top when one of the city's busiest intersections is named after you. Golden Dragon, whose lurid signage has stamped its name on a major Ring Road junction, is literally a Delhi icon. Red and gold interiors mimic a run-down faux-Chinese palace, and the "Chinjabi" food is equally suspect. The usual suspects – kung pao, schezuan and hot garlic sauce – dominate the menu, but there are more exotic ventures like the emperor pork ribs in honey, red wine and

Café Morrison

five spice powder. Just go for beer, really, out on the canopied balcony, floating above the clamour of south Delhi. *DDA Market, RBI Colony, Panchsheel, opposite Panchsheel Club (2696-9348); daily noon-midnight. Night out for two ₹1000.* ⊙

Keya

There's too rarely a distinction between a Delhi club and a drinking hole, and that's one reason why Keya's has struck gold. It's a bar-bar – elegant and supremely cosmopolitan with not one twitch of a personality disorder. The interior is dominated by a massive island-bar with an ebony base and a sweling, translucent, alabaster counter. It's the perfect place to explore Keya's creative cocktails, most of which have evolved from Delhi's street markets. The Keya Magique (₹400) is a paan mojito,

unwind yourself

LIGHTHOUSE
13

lounge
& bar

13-1st floor, mgf metropolitan mall, saket,
for reservation 9650622113

Keya

with bits of betel leaf and supari floating around the muddled vodka and a betel garnish that radiates aroma and flavour. One surprising drink is the Mast Guava (₹225), a tumbler filled to the brim with guava juice, vodka, a hint of lemon juice, chilli, chaat masala and black salt. The bar snacks are equally innovative, a bit like Indian tapas. The tawa-roasted lamb tikka (₹375) is succulent and beautifully marinated. Along with the cocktails, it will leave you shining as bright as the glow-worm bar. **DLF Promenade Mall**, *Nelson Mandela Marg, Vasant Kunj (95607-15533) Daily 7pm-1am. Night out for two ₹3,000.* ⑤

Kylin Lounge
Part-lounge (dark couches, low wooden tables, orange paper lamps) and part-restaurant (stiff-backed chairs, loud families), this spacious pan-Asian eatery is spread out over two floors and

has a large balcony for outdoor seating. Start your meal with some salmon and asparagus maki rolls served with a large dollop of wasabi and lots of scorchingly-sweet gari (shavings of pickled ginger). As you watch the afternoon morph into evening, you realise two things: one, unlimited sushi can leave you feeling nice and full; and two, beer and sushi make for a heady combination.
24 Basant Lok, first floor, Vasant Vihar (99111-59546). Sun noon-4pm. Sushi Sundays ₹ 2,500. ㊻

Olive
In 2007, a collective wail emanated across the capital when Olive was shut down, part of the government's overzealous sealing drive. Imagine the jubilation in 2010 when it reopened and seemed to have merely been stuck in a time-warp. It is as white – wicker furniture and table posies included – and softly lit as it always was. Still in place are the Isle-of-Capri-like pearly pebbles in the courtyard and the banyan tree overhead. And it's still not a place to go with light pockets. The goat cheese soufflé starter (₹425) is lighter than air, the charcoal mushrooms and Spanish artichokes (₹455) are delectable, and perfect washed down with a kiwi-strawberry margarita (₹450). A consistent favourite is Olive's thin-crust pizzas (from ₹595). Watch the beautiful people – and your tab.
One Style Mile, Mehrauli (2957-4444). Daily 7pm-1am. Night out for two ₹3,500. ㊼

DELHI BY AREA

Red Monkey

Red Monkey

Big enough to fit all your friends, small enough to make you feel right in the centre of things. Red Monkey can be alternately crowded or calm, but it's quickly swinging its way into the hearts of Delhi's bar-hoppers. On a busy night, it can feel like a party at someone's apartment. The cocktail menu is dotted with anecdotes and names; by the end of the night you'll know the owners, all their friends and their drink preferences.
47 Defence Colony Market, above Chilli Seasons (918108-08654). Daily noon-1am. Night out for two ₹2,500. ④⑨

The Zoo

With disco balls, laser lights, snakeskin-patterned walls and tables that double as mirrors, the Zoo is an exciting reminder that new-age disco has arrived. In addition to the usual spirits, they have six cocktails on its menu, served either by the glass (₹450) or by the pitcher (₹1,500). The mojitos definitely have mojo. The Zoo also offers snacks that are easy on the wallet. The most expensive item – garlic prawns – goes for a mere ₹350. What's also lovely is how it blurs the boundaries between indoors and outdoors. There are few places like the Zoo in Delhi that offer this kind of kitschy garden-fresh ambience. The over-the-top décor, great DJ and faux-jungle surroundings (electric-star-strewn palm trees border the outside patio area) make a trip out here worth your while.
Westend Marg, Garden of Five Senses, Said-ul-Ajaib (6557-6198) Daily 7.30pm-1am. Night out for ₹2,500. ④⑨

Turquoise Cottage

Although version 2.0 isn't a patch on the ambience of the original in Adhchini, the multiple levels here mean not everyone needs to stand beer-gut to beer-gut while they headbang to over energetic thrash metal bands. A perennial venue for the Rocktober festival, TCs is quite genuinely the cradle of Delhi rock.
47, Basant Lok Complex, above McDonald's (98182-09915). Daily noon to am. Night out for two ₹1,500. ⑤⓪

Arts & Leisure

Hard Rock Café

Space opens up in front of you as you walk in (₹250 entry fee when a band is playing), with a stage to the right and a glass-enclosed smoking room. The bar and stage face each other, leaving ample

Turquoise Cottage

space to rock out in. Naturally, there's a lot of music memorabilia, (all properly labelled to show what's what). There's a hefty cocktail list and menu, but the homemade nachos (₹425) complement your drinks just fine. *M-110 DLF Place Mall, first floor, District Centre, Saket (4715-8888). Daily noon-1am. Meal for two ₹2,000.* 51

Kairali spa

Authentic ayurvedic massages aren't easy to come by this far from Kerala. But there's always Kairali, the rare non-hotel spa offering some herbal TLC that won't break the bank (from ₹1000). *120 Andheria Modh, Mehrauli (6566-4447). Daily 9am-6pm.* 52

KHOJ Studios

The home of the Khoj International Artists Association is a whitewashed mini-haveli in the middle of the giant pothole that is Khirkee Extension. Light artists, visual DJs, fusion experiments and various other jugalbandi are given free rein here. On some nights the beer is free, but all nights are mind-bending anyway. *S-17 Khirkee Extension, near Sai Baba Mandir (6565-5874). Email interact@khojworkshop.org for the latest newsletter.* 53

Mocha Arthouse

The paintbox-bright décor at Mocha Arthouse draws simultaneous inspiration from extra-terrestrials and 1950s modernism, which gives it a cheerfully off-balance air. Inside, the art on the walls is always changing, ably curated by Delhi's B.L.O.T/ Quicksand collective. Arthouse also takes its claim as a space for the performing arts seriously. On any given night, you might find a classical guitar quartet, a film screening, a Bharatanatyam masterclass, a "turntablism" workshop or a sitar recital in progress. *167, Ground Floor, DLF Promenade, Vasant Kunj (4607-5631). Daily 11am-*

DELHI BY AREA

midnight. Alcohol served. Meal for two ₹1800. 🟤

Nature Morte

After it was founded in New York's East Village in 1982 and closed in 1988, Peter Nagy revived Nature Morte in New Delhi in 1997 as an itinerant gallery and a curatorial experiment. Since then, Nature Morte has become synonymous in India with challenging and experimental forms of art; championing conceptual, photographic, and installation genres within a commercial market that remains fixated on painting. It is widely considered Delhi's best-designed and most cutting-edge gallery. *A-1 Niti Bagh, opposite Kamla Nehru College (4174-0215). Mon-Sat 10am-6pm. Entry free.* 🟤

Mocha Arthouse

Tamaya spa

Tamaya's the preferred destination at the end of a long week (hey, a long week of sight-seeing counts, too). To combat the effects of Delhi's heat and dust, the anti-ageing tropical treatment and the tropical de-ageing salt mousse scrub are popular (both ₹3,500).

Nature Morte

Jaypee Vasant Continental, Vasant Vihar (2614-8800). Daily 8am-8pm. Jaypee Siddharth, 3 Rajendra Place (2576-0000). Daily 8am-8pm. ⑤⑥

The Living Room Café

Tired of the Punjabi pretension at so many Delhi establishments? Step into TLR, and exchange it for the hipster pretension of an indie musician's loft in New York. The two-storey-plus-rooftop is occupied by expats, sipping Sula like they don't care, graduates of Turquoise Cottage, college students, mediawalas and some would-be models wearing fedoras.

The fish and chips is good as is the kingfish steak.
31, Hauz Khas Village (4608-0533). Daily 11am-11pm. Meal for two ₹2,000. ⑤⑦

W+K Gallery

Voted one of the best designed galleries in Delhi by *Time Out* – after just three shows in as many months, this avant-garde advertising agency's space is also used to host exhibitions, workshops, readings, performances and film screenings.
Wieden+Kennedy, B-10, DDA Complex, Sheikh Sarai Phase I (4600-9595). ⑤⑧

Lado Sarai
DELHI'S NEW ART DISTRICT

Once known as Qila Rai Pithora, the capital of Prithviraj Chauhan, Lado Sarai is still crowded with carpet and furniture shops. But since 2007, nearly a dozen art galleries have appeared in the throng: Artoholics, Krishna's Collection, Ragini, Anant Art's two spaces, Art Eterne, Gallery Threshold, Art Motif, Artpilgrim and La Indaprastha Art Gallery, as well as the HQ of the online art portal Lantern of Art. Jindal Arts sells prints and knick-knacks ("specialists in Raja Ravi Varma prints", said the shop assistant), several shops sell painting supplies, and Take on Art magazine runs out of an office here. Now Lado Sarai is a central feature on the art map – serious buyers usually make the rounds of several galleries. **Exhibit 320** *F-320 Lado Sarai (4613-637). Mon-Sat 10.30am-6.30pm.* **Latitude 28** *F-208 Lado Sarai (4679-1111). Daily 11am-7pm.* ⑤⑨

Exhibit 320 gallery

DELHI BY AREA

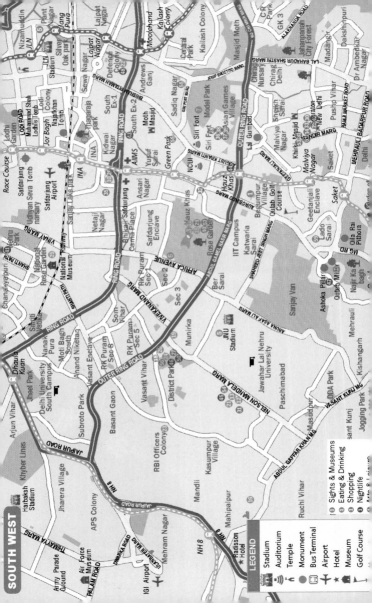

South East

Nizamuddin Dargah

The Bahà'i Temple

SOUTHERN COMFORT

The heart of southeast Delhi (what we're calling everything between the Bus Rapid Transport Corridor and the Yamuna) is not the vast fourteenth-century fortress of Tughlaqabad. Instead, it's a pair of graves, belonging to the Sufi saint Hazrat Nizamuddin Auliya and his creatively gifted disciple Amir Khusrau. This is today, as it was 700 years ago, one of the most revered sites in the city, the most thronged by devotees of every religion, a steady pulse of light through Delhi's many ruinations.

Of course, the space between the vital dargah of Nizamuddin and the dramatic ruins of Tughlaqabad is no longer filled with wheat-fields and tombs. It's filled with some of Delhi's best bars and restaurants, shops and art galleries. Its markets, for instance, range from the swanky-and-you-know-it N-Block of Greater Kailash I to the cyberpunk vision that is the Nehru Place computronics hub. The area is lively, varied and comfortable to explore, especially now that a new line of the Metro runs all the way down it.

Asola Bhatti Wildlife Sanctuary

Sights & Museums

Asola Bhatti Wildlife Sanctuary

Delhi has the second-to-largest number of bird species of any capital city, and the Asola Bhatti Sanctuary is a great place to see them. It's the largest plot of undisturbed Ridge forest left in Delhi, parts of it still resisting the invasion of the vilayati keekar tree imported by the British in 1915. Here you can look out for two rare birds – the Orphean warbler and the black redstart.
Near Karni Singh shooting range, Tughlaqabad (2604-2010). Daily 9.30am onwards; ₹50 per person. ❶

Baha'i Temple

One of the few examples of glorious Delhi architecture that's less than a few centuries old, the Baha'i house of worship, or Lotus Temple, was designed by the Iranian architect Fariborz

Sahba. It's cool in more ways that one, built around local principles of architectural cooling that have been in disuse for centuries. The temple is surrounded by pools, and blowers pull the cool air above them into the main prayer hall. The main structure is built of concrete, but between the concrete and the marble-cladding is a gap that acts as an insulating layer. As a result, the prayer hall stays incredibly comfortable through the year, without air-conditioning. There's a massive prayer hall at its heart, and even for those with no inclination to the spiritual, a few quite moments spent in silence here are energising. The Lotus Temple celebrates its silver jubilee in 2011.
Baha'i House of Worship, behind the Nehru Place bus terminal (2644-4035). ⊖ Nehru Place. Apr 1-Sep 30 Tues to Sun 9am-7pm; Oct 1-March 31 Tues to Sun 9.30am-5.30pm. Entry and parking free. ❷

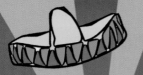

Watch this space

YOUR FRIENDLY NEIGHBOURHOOD BAR

Double Decker

Fridays: Bar Nights

Party all week with an awesome food menu, great cocktails and an elaborate liquor menu in the perfect retro setting.

At: E - 3, 3rd & 4th Floor, South Extension Part Two, New Delhi - 110049. Tel.: +91 11 4773 4400 +91 11 4773 44 44

the tasty tangles

CASUAL DINING. AUTHENTIC CHINESE.

Delhi:
Shop No. 305 / 306, 2nd Floor,
DLF Promenade Mall, Vasant Kunj,
Nelson Mandela Rd, New Delhi.
Tel: 011 41066000, +91 9717596501
Bengaluru:
Unit No. 204, 2nd Level, 4th Floor
Comet Block, UB City,
#24, Vittal Mallya Road, Bengaluru.
Mumbai:
Pinacle House, Plot No. 604, Ground Floor,
PD Hinduja Rd, Bandra (W), Mumbai.

Ghalib Museum

DELHI BY AREA

STADIUM Dr. Karni Singh Shooting Range
Spread over 72 acres, the Range has been divided into six parts – an indoor 10-metre range, an outdoor 25-metre range, a 50-metre range, a final range, trap and skeet range and a new armoury building.
Surajkund Road, Tughlaqabad. ❸

Ghalib Museum
Ghalib is Delhi's eternal poet laureate – he was a genius of the last Mughal court, and survived the devastation of the city by the British army in 1857. For the Ghalib fan, the academy has a one-room museum exhibiting his papers and other writings. Don't miss the displays of Ghalib's favourite food.
Ghalib Academy, Hazrat Nizamuddin West (2435-1098) Mon-Sat 11am-6pm. Entry free. ❹

Humayun's Tomb
This rather magnificent tomb

Humayun's Tomb

Nizamuddin Dargah

houses the grave of the second great Mughal, Humayun (Akbar's father). Said to be the model for the Taj Mahal, which was built by Humayun's great-grandson Shah Jahan, the sixteenth-century tomb is set among beautifully landscaped gardens, punctuated with water channels. It came to define the Mughal style of architecture, with its imaginative melding of Indian motifs with Persian and Central Asian techniques and styles (some of the smaller tombs around it, belonging to ministers, are even more architecturally curious). An evening visit here, with the kites wheeling overhead and the river in the background, should be an entrancing experience. Delhi's late-winter cultural highlight, the Jahan-e-Khusrau festival, brings the greatest singers in the Sufi tradition to perform here. *Lodhi & Mathura Roads, Nizamuddin East (2435-5275). Open daily, sunrise-sunset. Indians and SAARC nationals* ₹*10, others* ₹*250. Children below 15 free.* ⑤

Inayat Khan's dargah

Inayat Khan was a nineteenth-century Sufi pir, the only one whose following exists mainly outside South Asia. Few people in the lively and decrepit neighbourhood of the dargah of Inayat Khan even know it exists. Those who know it also know that qawwali is performed there every Friday, but prefer to leave it to *angrezi logon* (English people). This local disinterest should not discourage qawwali enthusiasts. The singing begins after the Friday evening prayer, around his grave. Mehraj Ahmed Nizami has been singing at the Inayati dargah for 40 years. Even if your experience of the music is secular, the ambience, the acoustics and the intimacy of the room make it uniquely personal and lovely. *127, Nizamuddin Basti (2435-0833). Qawwali on Friday evenings, timings vary.* ⑥

The Surajkund mela

Jahanpanah Forest

Quiet green spaces are a merciful respite from the chaos of New Delhi, and it is south Delhi's good fortune to have several. One of the largest, and most secret, is this centuries-old forest that stretches nearly 3km from the Sufi shrines at Chiragh Dilli to the ruined fort of Tughlaqabad (both also worth visiting).
Entrance from Greater Kailash II, opposite Don Bosco school. Timings 4-10am; 4-6pm. Entry free. ❼

Nizamuddin Dargah

The mausoleum of one of the world's most famous Sufi saints, Hazrat Nizamuddin Auliya, is also located in an area that has been continuously inhabited and revered since the thirteenth-century, when Dilli was only a city around the Qutb Minar. "Bustling" does not describe its

modern atmosphere: the dargah is visited by thousands every day, Muslims as well as people of other faiths. The tomb of Amir Khusro, who is credited with inventing qawwali and many other musical innovations, and Jahanara Begum (a beloved daughter of Shah Jahan) are nearby. Qawwali every Thursday is an essential Delhi tradition, which means it's getting a *little* overrun, and some people may prefer the qawwali at Inayat Khan's quieter dargah nearby. The other big draw in the area is the multitude of kebab joints, chief among them being Karim's.
Mathura Road, near Humayun's Tomb. Entry free. ⊖*Jangpura* ❽

Surajkund

Literally meaning "Lake of the Sun", this tenth-century reservoir has an amphitheatre-like embankment supposedly meant

Tughlaqabad Fort

for sun-worshipping. Two kilometers north of here lies the even more ancient eighth-century Anagpur Dam. Although mining in the area has severely affected the water supply in Surajkund, it still plays host to the Surajkund Mela every February, where craftspeople congregate to display their wares.
Baharpur village, Faridabad, past Charmwood Village. ❾

Tughlaqabad Fort

This is one of the most "obvious" secrets in a city dotted with the ruins of Mughal forts. Tughlaqabad doesn't appear on tour operators' itineraries, and the fort has been spared most of the trappings of hawkers or people offering to take your picture, so it's good for some wild monument-rambling. For most parts of the year, wild shrubbery surrounds the hillock on which the fort stands. But the high battlements and imposing fort walls resonate with the tales of how the third city of Delhi was built by Ghiyasuddin Tughlaq, and cursed by the Sufi saint Nizammudin Auliya, who said Tughlaq's city would soon be occupied by only jackals and Gurjars (a caste of herdsmen). So it came to be, and so it remains.
Mehrauli-Badarpur road, near Karni Singh shooting range. Daily 9.30am-6pm. ₹5 per person. ❿

Eating & Drinking

Culinaire

A little like a Thai dhaba, Culinaire serves up cheap, delicious Thai, Lebanese and Chinese food. The sidewalk seating is intimate but scarce, and the inside is tiny, which is why Culinaire's fortunes are built on delivery and takeaway. Their

Culinaire

Thai food is the best of the lot, made with almost-authentic – and more importantly – really fresh ingredients. We love the Thai green curry, as well as the vegetarian pad Thai (which has tofu and broccoli) to which (for a small price) prawns can be added. Culinaire's portions are huge and comforting, just what you need for a night in – or out. Especially lovely in the winter, when the staff brings out hot coals on grills.

1 Chandan Market, S-Block, Greater Kailash II (2921-2414, 2921-8050). Daily 12.30-3pm, 6.30-11pm. Meal for two ₹500. ⑪

Diva

Ritu Dalmia left London and Vama, her successful Indian restaurant there, to bring her true love, Italian cuisine, to Delhi. Like its owner and chef, Diva is relaxed, welcoming and serious about the freshest ingredients and the smoothest wines. Daily specials are good, the swordfish is classic and there's an eight to ten-course tasting menu. The fish dishes are fabulous; the salads fresh and light; the desserts delectable and the atmosphere

Diva

Indian Accent

The International Diner

cozy. A luxurious but not extravagant dining experience. *M-8A Greater Kailash-II, M Block Market; (2921-5673).Daily 12.30-3pm; 7.30-11pm. Major credit cards accepted. Alcohol served. Meal for two ₹3,500.* ⑫

Indian Accent

Owner Rohit Khattar's Indian and pan-Asian outlets in London (Tamarai and Sitaaray among them) have influenced the internationally inflected Indian food at this cosy-but-elegant restaurant in the boutique Manor Hotel. There's an attached bar and a veranda overlooking the lawn. The backbone of the cuisine is regional Indian food (from Kerala to Kashmir), but the spicing and presentation are completely global. Don't miss the foie gras-stuffed galawati: soft minced meat kababs with morsels of foie gras inside and a drizzle of strawberry and green chilli chutney. For mains, try the sweetish tamarind-

glazed New Zealand lamb shank, or the rice-crusted red snapper moily – and save room for dessert. If choosing seems too hard, there's an affordable tasting menu. *Manor Hotel, 77 Friends Colony (West) (2692-5151). Lunch noon-3pm; dinner 7-11pm. Meal for two ₹5,000. Tasting menu per person: dinner ₹1,900 (non-vegetarian), ₹1,800 (vegetarian); lunch ₹900 (non-vegetarian), ₹800 (vegetarian); wine add ₹1,000 per person (five half glasses).* ⑬

The International Diner

An "international diner" could only be the result of the current Delhi vogue for taking grubby, casual-dining institutions and gentrifying them into a whole new thing. TID has dark wood tables, stripey sofas and pouffe cushions and a glass-walled kitchen (no coffee-stained counter here). The menu gets pretty international too, with shawarma, pasta and banta, aside from "diner fries",

Kabul Restaurant

Coke floats, and classic diner specialties like all-day breakfasts. The very diner-ish mushroom duplex with Jack Daniel's barbecue sauce are excellent. A more elegant option is Norwegian pink salmon in white wine and dill sauce. *M-69, first floor, M-Block Market, Greater Kailash-I (4669-6140). Daily noon-11pm. Alcohol served. All credit cards accepted. Meal for two ₹1,500.* ⑨

Kabul Restaurant

The Afghans are the newest wave of refugees to make Delhi their home, and they've peppered this locality with community eateries. The delicious and stupor-inducing cuisine at Kabul will make you wonder how the Taliban are so active. Order the korma pulao, a heady misture of rice, raisins and mutton slivers, with large chewy meatball-like koftas as an accompaniment. Wash it down a

Malabar's

Le Café

A café that is able to achieve, in this city of climatic extremes, the kind of glorious outdoorsy-feel that restaurateurs in more temperate climes take for granted, deserves a round of applause. In terms of value for money, main courses here are a better bet than the snack-like sandwiches, which cost almost as much. If you're really starving, the risotto with spinach (₹280) is a good idea – creamy, tasty and very filling.
N-1, GK-I, N Block Market (third floor, above the Ravi Bajaj Showroom) (41731035). Credit cards accepted. Daily 11.30am-10pm.

glass of fragrant green tea.
Shop 4/8, Central Road, opposite Modi Pantry, Jangpura Bhogal (97113-19057, 96549-45016). Meal for two ₹300.

Lazeez Darbar

Lazeez is mostly a take-away joint, but has some seating, a TV and arctic air-con. The genial owners (brothers Kifayatullah and Salamatullah) are frequently on the premises to lead you through the menu of tandoori and Mughlai food. Try the brilliant mutton burra kababs and the signature gola kabab, made with chicken or mutton mince. The qormas are richly spiced but won't give you nightmares – sop them up with shirmal bread.
C-1/2 Jangpura B, next to Rajdoot Hotel (2437-4444). Daily 11.30am-4pm, 6.30pm-11.30pm. No alcohol served. No credit cards. Meal for two ₹500.

Malabar's

Rumour has it that Doña Juliana Dias da Costa was a Portuguese woman from Kerala who presided over Mughal emperor Bahadur Shah I's harem. Sarai Julena is named for her and, appropriately enough, it's now a Keralite enclave of sorts. Malabar's Kerala food selection includes fish fry, pothu (beef) curry and dry kappa biryani, puttu and kadala curry. The thali is very popular here, perhaps because of the quantity of heaped red rice and sambar. Nearby stands the sunnier space of Joys, which has a longer menu and more veggie options.
33B Sarai Julena, opposite Escorts Hospital. Ask for directions (6502-6147; 98186-15196). Daily 7.30am-10.30pm. Home delivery available. Meal for two ₹250.

Oh! Calcutta

Even the most exacting Bengali critic will find little to fault in this

The Yum Yum Tree

oasis of calm in the chaos of Nehru Place, exemplifying the credo that one must never rush one's food. Order the bekti (fried fish), which is crumb-fried and juicy. Once done picking through it, the kosha manhsho (mutton curry) accompanied by hot, fluffy luchis (like puris) is note-perfect. End it with some gurer payesh, a sticky, jaggery-based pudding. *HA-1, International Trade Tower, ground floor, Nehru Place (2646-4180). ⊖ Nehru Place. Daily noon-3pm; 7-11.15pm. Meal for two: ₹2,500* ⑬

The Yum Yum Tree
Pink Hello Kitty chandeliers bloom from the ceilings of the upbeat, stylish café and grill. The kaiten sushi conveyor-belt eliminates the need to pronounce what you're eating. Snatch up the asparagus-cucumber Philadelphia rolls, barbequed black mushroom rolls or crunchy mayo-and-mustard soused prawn rolls. *Community Centre, first floor, New Friends Colony (98100-02993) Daily noon-3.30pm; 7pm-midnight. Meal for two ₹2,000* ⑳

Shopping

Eureka!
Eureka! is Delhi's only bookstore exclusively for young readers. It's quite cheery, without the loud trendiness of a mall bookstore, and a great place to partake of the current boom in kids' publishing from Delhi. *6 Local Shopping Center, Narmada Market, opposite Don Bosco School, Alaknanda (2602-1092) Mon-Sat 10am-7.30pm* ㉑

Fab India
If you've coveted Indian ethnic-chic at stores like the Conran Shop in London or New York, here's your chance to buy the fabrics and crafts at one-tenth the price. Fabindia sources its products from more than 7,500 craftspeople and artisans around India, aiding entire communities. It's also definitive of the fashion-sense of India's urban intellectual. Their distinctive use of handloom weaving techniques, natural dyes, and both vivid and earthy colors have made their products both fashionable and desirable. Bear in mind that the fabrics usually require gentle washing and drip-drying. Sizing and quality are inconsistent, so it's best to try anything on before you buy it. Also visit **Anokhi** next door. *N-14 Greater Kailash I, (4669-3724) Daily 10.30am-8.30pm.* ㉒

DELHI BY AREA

Nehru Place

Nehru Place is the embodiment of the wilful and uncontrollable nature of urban development in India. What was meant to be a "focal point of cultural synthesis and… intellectual ferment" is today an phantasmagoric hub for small-scale and informal IT services, pirated software sales and hardware repairs. You will find pavement vendors selling items like printer toner cartridges, blank optical media, printer paper and pirated software CDs, between stray cattle and children begging. Actually worth a visit for the sensory shock, but more so if you need to buy a new memory card.

Outer Ring Road, near Kalkaji Mandir. ⊖ *Nehru Place* ㉓

cNehru Place

DELHI BY AREA

Shalom

Smoke House Grill

Nightlife

Shalom

This bar was instrumental in bringing lounge-culture to Delhi. When it opened, partygoers were completely enamoured with the pristine white interiors, creating a low-lit yet inviting atmosphere. It is lovely, soothing and womblike. Still going strong after a fair few years in Delhi's fickle nightlife market, it's not cheap (₹240 for a pint), but is still perennially packed thanks to a steady stream of regulars who will swear that Shalom is still and always the coolest lounge in town. If you're planning to eat, remembers to make reservations.

N-18 Greater Kailash 1, N Block Market (4163-2280). Daily 12.30-3.30pm; 7.30pm-midnight. Night out for two ₹2,000. ㉔

Smoke House Grill

Inspired by contemporary pop-art and the minimalist East Asian design ethic, Smoke House Grill attracts socialites, designers, expats, industrialists and anyone who's anyone in Delhi's fly-set since it opened in 2007. But besides the unique cold-smoking method (using fruity wood-smoke grills to flavour food and drink) and the cocktails, one of the restaurant's main draws is their exhaustive wine list. Besides going out of their way to pick some of the best "new world" wines (from countries like Chile, Argentina and South Africa), SHG also has its staff trained in the fineries of the art by a wine producer once a month.
North Wing, VIPPS Centre, Plot No. 2, LSC Masjid Moth, Greater Kailash II (4143-5530/31). Daily 7.30-11.30pm. Night out for two around ₹4,000. Major credit cards accepted. Alcohol served. **㉕**

Art & Leisure

Gallery Espace

Gallery Espace is today one of the most influential galleries in the city, frequently hosting experimental efforts in performance and video art, as well as some canonical modern work.
Level 1, 16 Community Centre, New Friends Colony (2632-6267). Mon-Sat 11am-7pm. **㉖**

Vadehra Art Gallery

The granddaddy of Delhi's art galleries has been so successful, they bought out the Grosvenor gallery in London – it's now called Grosvenor Vadehra. They also have the distinction of hosting the first ever Picasso exhibition inside India at their Okhla gallery.
D178 Okhla Phase 1, near Silvertone Motors Skoda Showroom (6547-4005); D40 Defence Colony (2461-5368). Mon-Sat 11am-7pm. **㉗**

Vadehra Art Gallery

West Delhi

The Jhandewalan
Hanuman Statue

The Pitampura TV Tower

GO WEST, PUTTAR

West Delhi is Punjabi Delhi, the region that proudly – and loudly – represents the capital's largest community. When Pakistan was partitioned from India in 1947, millions of refugees from Pakistani Punjab fled from the massacres and camped in Delhi, eventually making it their home. Punjabi brio and gregariousness are still two of the virtues that nobody disputes about Delhi. Them and Punjabi butter chicken.

West Delhi, which begins near Connaught Place and sprawls out west of the Ridge forest all the way to the marshy apartment-blocks of Dwarka, is one of the youngest regions in the city. It goes without saying that it's still pretty raw when it comes to culture. All that most visitors will see of West Delhi is what they look down on as their aeroplanes descend (for a closer aerial view, the Metro line runs elevated all the way to Dwarka). Despite its reputation as a cultural deadzone, the West still has some star curiousities, like the Pitampura Dilli Haat and one of the world's rare toilet museums.

Sights & Museums

Adventure Island

At the north-western end of
the Metro line is Delhi's only
full-on amusement park, with
22 imported rides apparently
obtained from the same people
who set up Disneyworld. Only
two of these are water-based, the
rest are fun the year round. Our
favourite is the sidewinder. Once
you're strapped in, it begins to
gently swing from side to side,
and within a few seconds you're
swung up high enough to have
a view of the entire park, right
before the carousel starts turning
your world into a dizzy blur.
All that's missing is a seriously
scary roller coaster. Rohini is a
long way out, though.
*Sector 10, Rohini, near Rithala
Metro station (4704-1111,
2757-4061). Rithala. Daily
noon-9pm. Adults and children
₹400, students ₹350. Snacks
cost extra.* ①

Adventure Island

Air Force Museum

Hidden off the Dwarka road
behind the domestic airport
terminal, the museum of the
Indian Air Force is a contender
for Delhi's best kept secret. The
hangar and the outdoor apron

Air Force Museum

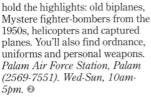

Sulabh International
Museum of Toilets

Tribal Museum

hold the highlights: old biplanes, Mystere fighter-bombers from the 1950s, helicopters and captured planes. You'll also find ordnance, uniforms and personal weapons. *Palam Air Force Station, Palam (2569-7551). Wed-Sun, 10am-5pm.* ❷

Sulabh International Museum of Toilets

There's Emperor Shah Jahan's peacock throne, and then there's the other kind of throne. The latter is the star at this museum in Mahavir Enclave, a long-ish Metro ride away from central Delhi on the Dwarka line. Built by the Sulabh foundation, which aims to bring toilet facilities to the millions of urban Indians who have no access to them, the museum charts the evolution of the commode: from the chamber pot to squat toilets to the "Western" toilets we know today. Displays include ornate porcelain

toilets from Austria, a model of a French portable commode that was disguised as a bookcase, and much more. The museum is amusing and informative, and you don't need to spend a penny. *Sulabh Bhawan, Mahavir Enclave, Palam Dabri Marg (2503-1518), Open Mon-Sat 10am-5pm. Admission free.* ❸

Tribal Museum

Clothes, weapons, medicinal herbs, jewellery and other traditional artefacts belonging to the tribal communities of India. Set up by the Bharatiya Adimjati Sevak Sangh,the museum includes a series of dioramas depicting scenes from tribal life and households. *Thakkar Bapa Sadan, Dr Ambedkar Marg, behind Jhandewalan Metro station (2752-5492). ⊖ Jhandewalan. Mon-Sat (excluding second Sat) 11am-5pm. ₹5.* ❹

Roshan Di Kulfi

Eating & Drinking

Amravathi

If you aren't brave enough to face the Andhra Bhavan peak hour rush, head out to Amravathi. It's best for lunch when you can opt for a thali and add on some fried fish or mutton dishes. It's not quite as perfect as Andhra Bhavan, but there are many more options on the menu, including some very competent fish curries. Stock up on speciality groceries at the South Indian supermarket in the basement on your way out. *18/2 Arya Samaj Road, WEA Karol Bagh (4353-2828). ⊖Jhandewalan. Daily 6.30am-10.30pm. No alcohol served. All major credit cards accepted for bills above ₹200. Meal for two ₹500.* ❺

Roshan Di Kulfi

Roshan di Kulfi is the social heart of the Karol Bagh market. This place is full no matter what time of day you visit, so always be prepared to watch over the seated patrons like a hawk and swoop down on a seat as soon as they vacate one. Next you have to place the order and then leave it up to the waiter's discretion of how early or late you will be served. They have a variety of options for breakfast, and snacks and chaat that include gol gappe, raj kachori and paneer tikka. But the highlight of each meal is the faluda kulfi (₹45), kulfi topped with sweet, rose-water vermicelli. Better than it sounds (or looks). *2816/18, Ajmal Khan Road, near Mehrasons, Karol Bagh (2872-4230). Daily 9am-11pm. Meal for two ₹150* ❻

Sahni Bhojan Bhandar

Situated in a narrow lane – flanked by large kadhai pans, wok-like patilas and a wide aunty at the cash counter – Sahni started as a pavement stall 50 years ago, and became a full-fledged dhaba in 1985. Although crammed with hungry men, it's entirely female-friendly. If you choose to skip the sizeable vegetarian menu and the more exotic meat offerings (kheema kaleji – kidney mince – and so on), settle for what most people seem to be eating: meat curry. The half-plate pool of curry with two pieces of meat, accompanied by thick-cut onions and lime and served with hot, crisp tandoori parathas is delicious. The meat is tender, the spice medium-high and the coriander not overpowering. Build up an appetite before you get here because an entire meal causes only ₹63 worth of damage. This little late-night joint is more than a place to eat – it's a social service.

2157/B-2 Guru Arjun Nagar, near Satyam Cineplex, Patel Nagar (2570-9987; 98737-86020). ⊖ Shadipur. Daily 11am-4pm; 6pm-2.30am ⓐ

Shopping

Tihar Haat

Tihar Jail is India's foremost "model" prison, subjecting its inmates to a range of reform programmes from vipassana meditation to baking. So it shouldn't be such a surprise to find Tihar Haat, the jailhouse store, outside the main gate of Central Jail 1. This is a one-stop shop for all your prison-product needs. Every day, the Tihar bakery churns out 1,500 loaves of bread – not just the plain white but multigrain and brown bread –besides 300 kgs of chips, 800 kgs of snacks like aloo bhujia and 100 kgs of biscuits. It began with biscuits and dresses, but TJ's has diversified into a multi-product operation. Women inmates busy themselves making beauty products, covers for wine and champagne bottles, candles, pottery, pickles and

Tihar Haat

Photoink

papads. TJ's "freedom factory" has also earned an ISO 9002 certification – a stamp of approval for A-grade products (though that's not beyond dispute). New programmes include a shoe factory where Swati Mehrotra trains a batch of ten inmates twice in week, and a hair academy at Jail No 2 run by Amzad Habib, son of famed stylist Javed Habib. Don't be too shy about buying something from here – it's unlikely your cake will have a nail file in it.
Near Jail No 1, Jail Road, Hari Nagar (2852-2120 for bulk orders and information). ⊖ *Tilak Nagar. Online shopping portal expected to open Oct 2010; visit www.tiharprisons.nic.in.* ❽

Arts & Leisure

Photoink
Essentially a creative lateral off Devika Daulet-Singh's photo agency by the same name, the Photoink gallery regularly hosts some of the most provocative photography shows in the city. Spread over 3500 square feet, Photoink represents young photographers at their primary gallery, but also holds exhibitions of illustrious guests, including Martin Parr and Lord Snowdon.
Hyundai MGF Building, Ground Floor, 1 Jhandewalan, Faiz Road (2875-5940, 2875-5941). Monday-Saturday 11am-7pm, Sunday 12pm-7pm. Closed on national holidays. ❾

Gurgaon

Gurgaon's posh residential sprawl

The Kingdom of Dreams

ALL ABOUT THE MALL

It's been a long time since Delhi thought of itself as among the most genteel and cultured cities in the world. But the unreal, mall-clad landscape of Gurgaon still makes any Dilliwala feel like a member of the Mughal court in comparison. Just a sleepy provincial township until two decades ago, Gurgaon has grown on the steroids of lax planning and plenty of money, and today it's a jumble of futuristic towers, chaotic highways and dusty, vacant expanses. But its undeniably on the rise, happy to rival Delhi in the quality of its shopping, restaurants and nightlife.

Having Gurgaon is like having a younger brother who eats too much, works out too much, brags a little bit too much, gets into brawls, but knows how to have a really good time. Besides, we know the crazy energy is just a younger, amplified version of what Delhi grew up on in the first place.

One of the world's
best new restaurants
- *Condé Nast Traveller*

Dappled sunlight on soft armchairs.
A white pebbled courtyard punctuated
by bougainvillea. A generously stocked
bar. And great Med-inspired food.

Welcome to a space so stunning that
Condé Nast Traveller voted it one of
the world's best new restaurants.

Drop in and discover the capital's best
kept secret.

olive
BAR & KITCHEN
World's best new restaurants
Condé Nast Traveler

Olive Bar & Kitchen, One Style Mile, Mehrauli, New Delhi – 30.
Phone: +91 11 29574444 / 9810235472.Tel.: (011) 46040404 / 99711 44455.
www.olivebarandkitchen.com. Join the 'Olive at the Qutub' group on Facebook.

Gurgaon

Kingdom of Dreams

The Kingdom of Dreams is the happy lovechild of Dilli Haat (p134) and Las Vegas. The buff-pink mock-sandstone palace holds two theatres, food, culture and shopping complexes, and a "cinema lounge". But it's more than just a theme park – it's a huge, clever, outré hallucination of modern India, folded into an air-conditioned box and roofed with a painted blue sky. Nautanki Mahal is an 850-seat entertainment centre where Bollywood-themed mega-musicals are performed. The ShowShaa Theatre hosts mythological productions. But the show-off centrepiece is Culture Gully, where 14 Indian states and cities are represented in show kitchens, restaurants, bars and retail shops ranged along a climate-controlled central boulevard. Additionally, visitors (and people trying to send a message to obtuse partners) can stage their own Bollywood-style mock-wedding.

Sector 29, Gurgaon (0124-4528000). Tue-Sun 1pm-1am. Culture Gully Rs 750 per person (Rs 100 entry; Rs 50 deposit). **❶**

Sultanpur Bird Sanctuary

Delhi's birdlife ranges from floppy-chinned pelicans to pink flamingos who come visiting each year, adding to the population of parrots, storks, sparrow, ravens, kites and the royal (and protected) peacock. Serious birdwatchers head out to Sultanpur, especially in winter, when the park receives thousands of migratory birds. The sanctuary has raised machans (watchtowers) at various points on the grounds, and there's an education center with books, films and slides. Consider staying overnight at the park's Rosy Pelican guesthouse. *The park is 50km from Delhi and 15km from Gurgaon on the Gurgaon-Farrukh Nagar Road (0124-2015670).* **❷**

Sultanpur Bird Sanctuary

B
ERC
O'S

BERCO'S®
CHINESE 'N THAI RESTAURANT
AND BAR

NOT YOUR TRADITIONAL CHINESE RESTAURANT.

ConnaughtP lace   Noida   Janakpuri   KamlaN agar   Dwarka   Pitampura
Rohini   PreetV ihar   RajouriG arden   Gurgaon   Faridabad   Amritsar

G-2/43,MiddleCircle,ConnaughtPlace,NewDelhi-110001
Tel.:43731111,Email:bercos@vsnl.com

Bernardo's

Eating & Drinking

Bernardo's

Bernardo's was the first place to serve authentic Goan food in the capital and its still the only one. The salivating faithful have followed from their first outlet in Mehar Chand Market to its bright new spot in Super Mart 1. Not one of them would dare compare it to the shacks in Goa. Tuck into some vindaloo (₹260), pork marinated and cooked in roasted Goan spices. Recipes have been handed down through the generations – the only concession is that all meats and fish are boneless. *B-229 Super Mart-1, DLF Phase-IV, Gurgaon (0124-6518323); Wed-Mon, 1-3.30pm, 7.30-10.30pm. Meal for two ₹1,000.* ❸

Great Indian Kebab Factory

This Delhi institution has long been the favourite of those who want to eat fancy kababs at fairly fancy prices – and they're very

good kababs, and in unlimited quantities. The set menu changes daily, you simply declare yourself non-vegetarian or vegetarian, and the food begins to arrive, course by wonderful course. Ignore the confused attempt at rustic chic (exposed brick walls and blue glass lamps that look like rolled-up umbrellas). A classic combination – galouti kabab (spiced roundels of minced mutton made tender with papaya) and ulte tawe ki roti (a sweet, lightly oiled chapati made on the back of the pan) – cannot be recommended highly enough. *Park Plaza Hotel, B-Block, Phase I Sushant Lok, Gurgaon (0124-4150000). Daily 12.30-3pm, 7pm-midnight. Alcohol available. Meal for two ₹ 4,500.* ❹

Hao Shi Nian Nian

This Gurgaon-based Sichuan specialist was starting to make New Delhi look passé. Master chef Mike Li Wei heads the open-

The timeless voyage continues ...

With a network spread across more than 30 cities worldwide, Time Out has come to represent 'the spirit of the city' across the globe.

The combination of a unique approach to editorial content, coupled with honest, unbiased reviews and cutting-edge design have symbolized the success of Time Out Mumbai, the fortnightly magazine on Art, Entertainment and Culture, since its inception in 2004.

And the same ease of breathing the city is reflective in Time Out Delhi capturing the heart of Delhiites.

In India, Time Out is now expanding its footprints with Time Out Bengaluru reaching out to as much as the nightlife enthusiastic as to the art connoisseur.

The incomparable teams of local experts across these 3 cities continually provide up-to-date information and critically sharp commentary on the Art, Entertainment and Cultural life.

So go on! Pick up your copy today !

Paprika Media
PUBLICATIONS

Life. Unlimited.

Gurgaon

plan kitchen, and his team of three chefs – also imported from Sichuan – includes a dim sum chef. The Shanghai steamed mini-buns are a juicy combination of minced chicken and spring onions, encased in a delicate opaque skin. Plump shrimp wrapped in translucent dumplings match any global standard for dim sum, while the spring onion cakes are startlingly delicious. This is how God made them: thin and partly crusty outside, but doughy-light within.

Hao Shi Nian Nian

There's an extensive wine list and a stage for live music. Hao Shi Nian Nian means "long live good things", so you can keep repeating it out loud as you leave.

Central Plaza, *Golf Course Road, Gurgaon (0124-4258888). Daily 12.30-3pm, 7pm-12.30am. Meal for two ₹3,000.* ⑤

Punjab Grill

Jiggs Kalra, legendary food writer, food historian and chef, designed Punjab Grill's menu, which draws on Jiggs' decades of experience and research into kababs. Everything you'd expect – butter chicken (gravy strained several times to make it smooth and velvety), dal makhani, Pindi chana, sarson da saag and makke ki roti (creamed mustard leaves and cornmeal bread) – all present, slightly tweaked and redone. Without employing the flamboyant fusion techniques of other haute Punjabi establishments (alcohol in your appetisers, anyone?), Kalra's up-to-the-minute innovation is backed by giant, village-sized portions and authentic knowledge of the food from both sides of the

Punjab Grill

Howzatt

border. Don't be alarmed by the green shotglass at the end of it all. It's a shot of liquified paan. ***Ambience Mall***, *third floor, Gurgaon (93115-20734). Daily 11am-11pm. Alcohol served. All major cards accepted. Meal for two* ₹*1,800.* ⑥

Shopping

Malls are to Gurgaon what tombs and mosques are to Delhi – definitive and everywhere. The town and the malls can even seem co-branded, because the Delhi Land Fund, which built most of Gurgaon and stamped various residential enclaves with the name DLF, also built the largest number of malls here. There are also several specialty shopping centres, like the flashy Gold Souk Mall. That apart, the shopping is almost identical in every mall. Most include a multiplex cinema, a food court and a crowd-pulling discount store like Big Bazaar. Just ₹100 for four boxer shorts? Hooray! The real draw is the

stand-alone bars and restaurants, which have willy-nilly ended up inside malls.

The side of the Mehrauli Gurgaon road, meanwhile, is worth checking out for replica antique furniture and other curios. Most of it is tacky, but you never know what you'll find on the gypsies' carts, which sell iron-worked candle-stands and other such souvenirs.
⊖ *MG Road* ❼

Nightlife

Howzatt

Howzatt was the country's first microbrewery pub with a head for cricket. A team of microbiologists led by masterbrewer SK Kohli craft 250 litres of fresh beer a day. The names of the beers keep up the pitch: the doosra is their lightest beer, with a distinctive, crisp taste. The googly is the light-bodied malted wheat beer and the bouncer is a dark brew with a bitter-sweet balance derived from roasted malt and

DELHI BY AREA

Gurgaon

Istanblu

DELHI BY AREA

hops. The barley comes pre-germinated and malted to the brewery, where it is milled, then brewed. Beer samples are offered on a cricket bat-shaped tray, with the last shot glass holding the barley, so you can see where beer comes from.
Galaxy Hotel, NH-8, near 32nd Milestone, Gurgaon (0124-4565000). Daily 1pm-1am. Night out for two ₹2,000. ⑧

Istanblu

A spacious and comfortable lounge option with dim lighting and pastel-coloured wallpaper, Istanblu does some fantastic cocktails (all at a flat ₹275) while the appetisers are large enough to serve as meals. Try the shish touk (₹275); the chicken is soft enough to melt in your mouth. Great stuff to line your stomach with, because the affordable beer (₹100) ensures you won't stop at just one pint.
The Trinity Residency, SCO 36, Sector 14, Gurgaon (0124-

4268845). Daily 11am-midnight. Ladies' nights on Saturdays: some drinks free for women until 10pm. Night out for two ₹1,000. ⑨

Jolly Rogers

While MG Road is a fair hop away from Maui, you can project

Jolly Rogers

yourself right into the Polynesian isles thanks to Jolly Rogers' tiki-bar décor – and its liquor selection of more candy-coloured tropical concoctions than Barbie's bar cabinet. Their appropriately rum-heavy cocktail menu abounds with drinks whose selling point is alcoholic strength. Most drinks brag at least a trio of mixed shots. The crow's-nest vantage point means that there isn't even an echo of the traffic beneath.
Time Tower, *10th floor, MG Road, Gurgaon (0124-4333555) Daily noon-midnight. Night out for two ₹ 3,500.* ⑩

Terroir
Terroir has an extensive list of international mid-priced wines. The décor melds circular '70s shag rugs and sleek silver lighting with massive sea-anemone-esque lamps in jewel tones. Try the crisp, dry Danzante Pinot Grigio (₹490) or

Terroir

a full-bodied Lindemans Bin 50 Shiraz (also ₹490). A modest beer selection is compensated by a longer list of quirky cocktails like the pleasingly pulpy kiwi margarita (₹295).
Galaxy Hotel, *NH-8, Sector 15, Gurgaon (0124-4032222). Daily 7.30pm-11.30pm. Night out for two ₹2,000.* ⑪

Arts & Leisure

Devi Art Foundation
An initiative of Anupam Poddar, considered the city's foremost contemporary art collector, the foundation showcases cutting-edge art practice to the public – like an exhibition of Pakistani contemporary art considered to be the best show in Delhi in 2010. This includes elaborate video installations, photography, sculpture, and (increasingly popular) mixed media works, all displayed within a brick and steel industrial-style gallery.
Sirpur House, *Plot 39, Sector 44, behind Apparel House, Gurgaon (0124-4888111). ⊖ HUDA City Centre. Tue-Sun 11am-7pm.* ⑫

Epicentre
A branch of the India Habitat Centre, the major cultural and institutional complex in central Delhi. It is making the first valiant attempts to host cultural perform-ances in its Gurgaon auditorium. It also contains an art gallery and a pleasant cafeteria. Still a little neglected and tumbleweed-ish, except when a festival is planned.
Apparel House, *Sector 44, Gurgaon (0124-2715200). ⊖ HUDA City Centre.* ⑬

DELHI BY AREA

East + Noida

Gautam Buddha statute

**Veiled statues at the
Gautam Buddha Park**

ACROSS THE RIVER

Often considered the low-rent end of Delhi, because it's across
the Yamuna river, East Delhi was a sprawl of working-class and
middle-class urbania until Noida – the New Okhla Industrial
Development Area – was carved out of the neighbouring state
of Uttar Pradesh.

Over just a few years, Noida transformed from onion-fields into
one terminus of the roaring, soaring, hyper-commercial National
Capital Region (the other, even more hyperbolic, is Gurgaon to
the west). It has countless shopping malls, call centres and the
wildest superclub in the National Capital Region. It is also home
to Film City, the hub for Delhi's news channels and soap opera
studios. Its growth is uncontrolled, spilling into ecologically
precious areas like the Yamuna's floodplain and turfing up
farming communities further east. But above all, the *Yamuna
paar* (Across-the-River) is still a residential suburb that testifies
to the numbers of people who demand their piece of Delhi.

Akshardham temple

Sights & Museums

Akshardham Temple

A monument to piety or ostentation? You decide. Controversially built on the Yamuna floodplain, and recorded as the largest Hindu temple in the world, Akshardham has swiftly become a must-see on the tourist circuit. Join massive crowds of devotees and daytrippers as they lap up its Disneyland-like attractions, including a "boat ride" through triumphalist ancient Indian, animatronic tableaux and a giant-screen film about Swaminarayan, the founder-deity of the sect that built the temple.

Or you could simply marvel at the ornately carved sandstone-and-marble structure, and the 326m-long pink sandstone frieze of massive elephants wrapped around its base. The place has strict security rules: No electronic items are allowed in the complex, including mobile phones or cameras. Go with some time to spare, because it takes three hours to view the temple, its gardens and exhibitions.

Indraprastha Park

National Highway-24, near
Noida More (2201-6688).
⊖ Akshardham. Open Oct-Mar
daily 9am-6pm; Apr-Sept daily
9am-7.30pm. Exhibitions daily
9am-5.30pm. Temple admission
complex free; exhibitions Indian
Rs 125; Rs 200 others. ❶

Indraprastha Park
Launched in 2000 by the Delhi
Development Authority, the
₹160-million project was aimed at
converting a 34-hectare landfill
into a green patch. This didn't
happened very efficiently, but it's
green now and the park is open to

Café $tyle

DELHI BY AREA

the public. It's a relaxing spot in which to watch the real Delhi relaxing. There's a modern Buddhist stupa and, thank god, a great view of Humayun's Tomb from the park.
Outer Ring Road, near Nizamuddin Bridge exit. Sunrise-8.30pm. Entry free. ❷

STADIUM Yamuna Complex
The Commonwealth Games venue for archery and table tennis.
⊖ *Karkardooma, Jhilmil, Anand Vihar.* ❸

Eating & Drinking

Café $tyle
This new café manages to blend in with its environment while just rising above it, with a cheery outdoor patio overlooking the dusty Sector 18 market. The Burgerrabia is good for a quick but rather substantial bite. A pita-like chapati, speckled with roasted sesame seeds, is piled up with juicy strips of buff tenderloin, little bits of marinated chicken, laced with lettuce and

**Cooking rolls at the
Sector 18 Market**

smeared with hummus and onion-jam. Another proto-pita is placed on top. Delicious, filling and reasonably-priced.

K-1 Dharam Palace, Sector 18, Noida (95120-4548472). Daily 8am-midnight. Meal for two ₹ 1,000. ④

Shopping

Sector 18

Known colloquially as Atta Market, you can get everything from jewellery and junk food to shoes and lampshades here. Even though it's surrounded by malls – Centrestage to the west, the Great India Place to the south and SAB Mall to the north – Atta's wide lanes and convenient parking attract more visitors. Plenty of bars, restaurants, coffee-shops and ice cream parlours, but the real excitement is the mutton-roll vendors who show their skills at night. Nothing remains of the Atta village.

Sector 18, Noida. ⑤

Flluid

Nightlife

Flluid

At first glance, this bar's all very Jetsons: light, bright, airy and space-age, with moulded white and silver leather seating snaking around the two-level space, punctuated with round white tables and bright speckled walls. Flluid has an actual club vibe, though there's food being served in addition to the extensive and eclectic drinks menu. The specialty cocktail, the fluid kick, is a lethal blend of gin, vodka, Old Monk, tequila, blue curacao and Red Bull (₹350).

Mosaic Hotel, *C-1 Sector 18, Noida (0120-402-5000). Mon-Fri 2pm-10.45pm, Sat-Sun 2pm-11.45pm. Night out for two ₹1,500.* ❻

Quantum

Quantum, which calls itself Delhi's first "superclub", appeared in the place of Elevate, Delhi's original and legendary clubbing sensation. Its primary pull is

either the technical details of the mainstage (with a 600-capacity bodysonic dancefloor, built over sub-woofers)

or the impressive line-up of international DJs they regularly bring in. Quantum has all the sheen and surging walls of sound you'd expect after all the superclub-talk, fuelled by five separate drinks bars and a "neutralise" bar near the exit, which pours fresh juices and rehydrating non-alcoholic drinks into party-people who need to sober up. There's no better place to get a glimpse of the city's young, rabid dance music subculture.

Fifth floor, Centre Stage Mall, Sector 18, Noida (95120-4364611). Night out for two ₹ 4,500. ●

Cinemas

PVR Spice
Address *I-2, Sector 25A*
Tel Enquiry *95120-4389000*
Website *pvrcinemas.com*
Credit Card *Yes*
Facilities *Snack Bar, wheelchair access, home delivery facilities at extra charges.* **TIP** *5 shows daily.*

Wave Cinemas
Location *Noida Address L-1,Centre Stage Mall, Sector 18*
Enquiry Tel *95120-4364623*
Advance Booking Tel *95120-4364666*
Website *wavecinemas.com*
Credit Card *Yes*
Films *Hindi, English, Children*
Facilities *Snack Bar, wheelchair access.* **TIP** *2 shows daily.*

Arts & Leisure

Kiran Nadar Museum of Art
Headed up by Kiran Nadar, the KNMA has one of the largest private collections of modern and contemporary art from the Subcontinent, spread over 13,000 sq ft. The gallery-museum was created with the initial idea of providing a creative outlet to the 65,000-strong staff at Nadar's husband's company, HCL. Artists displayed here include FN Souza, MF Husain, VS Gaitonde, Tyeb Mehta, Arpita Singh and Jogen Chowdhury as well as younger contemporaries like Subodh Gupta and Atul Dodiya.
Plot 3A, Sector 126, Noida. ⊖ Botanical Gardens. Tue-Sun 10am-6.30pm. ●

Essentials

The ITC Maurya

The Shangri-La

Hotels

Hotel rooms in Delhi tend to be expensive, given comparable facilities elsewhere in the world. Whenever you book a room, make sure you ask for the total price including taxes, as many hotels and restaurants add a hefty luxury tax to your bill. Forts, palaces and historic buildings all over the country have been converted into hotels. Unfortunately, there is no definition or control over what gets labeled as a heritage hotel. Many are wonderful places, but as with old buildings anywhere, can have problems with plumbing, steep staircases, ventilation and so on. Ask plenty of questions to find out what kind of room you are getting before you book.

There are Bed & Breakfast options in the city where rooms in a family's home are rented out to tourists at a more reasonable rate. Those recognised by the Delhi Tourism department are listed on www.delhitourism.nic.in/delhitourism/accommodation/bed_breakfast.jsp; many also have their own websites. While they allow tourists to live with and engage with locals, there is a variation in quality and facilities. This section lists some varied options for accommodation across the city.

Central Delhi

The Shangri-La
19 Ashoka Road, Connaught Place (4119-1220). Visit www.shangri-la.com. $$$$
Located bang in the middle of Central Delhi, the view from any side of the Shangri-La is spectacular: India Gate and Rashtrapati Bhavan are always in sight, and on a clear day, you can even see the Qutab Minar in the distance. Luxurious rooms are tastefully furnished, with wood-panelled closets, desk, chair, couch and many mirrors. A glass partition separates the bathroom from the bedroom, making rooms appear more spacious. 19 Oriental Avenue is among the top run of East Asian restaurants in Delhi. The spa, lit by candles, has running water flowing through every room – it's a wonderful place to relax and indulge.

Imperial
Janpath (2334-1234). Visit www.theimperialindia.com. $$$$
The fragrance of jasmine wafts around you, there's soothing piano music in the background and opulence is everywhere: in the marble floors, the cisterns full of flower petals, the fountains and the chandeliers. It all adds up to an air of luxury harking back to a different era. Most of the lobbies and restaurants in the Imperial are furnished in a colonial British style, with white couches and armchairs, plush carpets, and old sepia-toned photographs from the days of the Raj. Tea and coffee are taken in the Atrium, which seems more like the set of a Henry James novel than a modern-day hotel. In the midst of all that Indo-British luxury, guests will also find more modern amenities, from a Chanel store to a beauty salon and barbershop. The Imperial's

Imperial

ESSENTIALS

Name and address of the property

The Corbett Hideaway
Zero Garjia Dhikuli
Ramnagar, Distt. Nainital,
Uttrakhand - 244715
Ramnagar, Distt. Nainital,
Uttarakhand

The Riverview Retreat
Zero Garjia Dhikuli
Ramnagar, Distt. Nainital,
Uttrakhand - 244715
Ramnagar, Distt. Nainital,
Uttarakhand

Hideaway River Lodge
Village Jammun, Reserve
Forest, Corbett National
Park, Uttrakhand - 244715
Ramnagar, Distt. Nainital,
Uttarakhand

The Naini Retreat
Ayarpetta Slopes, Mallital,
Nainital-263001
Nainital, Uttarakhand

The Haveli Hari Ganga
Pilibhit House, 21 Ramghat
Haridwar –249401
Haridwar, Uttarakhand

Sun n Snow Inn
Near Ana-Shakti Ashram,
Kausani Bageshwar
Uttarakhand- 263639
Kausani, Bageshwar,
Uttarakhand

**The Himalayan View
Retreat**
Malla Ramgarh, Distt
Nainital- 263137
Ramgarh, Nainital,
Uttarakhand

The Camp 5 Elements
02nd Suspension Bridge,
Sinthali Village, Kaudiyala,
District Pauri, Rishikesh-
249192
Kaudiala, Rishikesh

The Earls Court
Opp. Balika Vidhya Mandir,
Near Balrampur House,
Mallital Nainital-263001
Nainital, Uttarakhand

The Fort Unchagaon
Village-Uncha Gaon
Garhmuketashwar, Distt-
Bulandshahar- 202398
Garhmuketashwar, Distt-
Bulandshahar

Chardham Camp (Barkot)
Yamunotri Road Near
Dobata, District- Uttarkashi-
249141
Barkot, Uttarkashi

Chardham Camp (Maneri)
6 Km. Ahead Maneri Dam
C/o Himalayan Water Sangh
Distt –Uttarkashi-249194
Maneri, Uttarkashi

Chardham Camp (Harsil)
Kalp Kedar Mandir, Village-
Dharali, P.O Harsil Distt.
Uttarkashi- 249335
Harsil, Uttarkashi

**Chardham Camp
(Guptakashi)**
3.KM Ahead Guptakashi,
Kedarpuram, P.O-Guptakashi
Distt. Rudraprayag- 246439
Guptkashi, Rudraprayag

**Chardham Camp
(Joshimath)**
Near Joshi Vidhalay,
Joshimath Distt. Chamoli-
246443
Joshimath, Chamoli

**Punjab & Sind Awas
(Kedarnath)**
Kedarnath

Vishranti Resort
Madhyant Farms, Lower
Kandolli (Prem Nagar)
Dehradun

The Xanadu Resort
Village & Post Office :
Majkhali Via Ranikhet,
District Almora, Uttrakhand -
244715
Ranikhet

The Light House of Aguada
Villa no B-27 at AGUADA
ANCHORAGE, Sinquerim,
Candolim, Goa - 403515
Goa

The Manor Kashipur
Near Chaiti Chauraha,
Bazpur Road, Kashipur-
244713
Kashipur

magnificent restaurant, 1911, extends over three connected areas: bar, formal dining area and turquoise-pillared veranda, overlooking a lawn. If the imperial architecture, wicker chairs, impeccable collection of photos and prints and unusual floral arrangements aren't impressive enough, 1911's 15-page wine list should keep you occupied.

Old Delhi

Maidens Hotel

7 Sham Nath Marg (2397-5464). Visit www.maidenshotel.com. $$-$$$

This Civil Lines landmark has been around since 1903. The grandeur of the building has survived, while the amenities have been updated. High ceilings, huge windows, faded paintings all lend an old-fashioned charm – you can almost see the ghosts of imperial officers. Start with a drink at the Cavalry Bar, hop across to the Old City or Delhi University by cycle-rickshaw, return and take a swim in the quiet pool. Suites (regular rooms aren't as nice) are spotless and modern, with enormous bathrooms, but note that windows are frosted and overlook a communal veranda. By Delhi standards, for what you're getting, the Maidens is pretty affordable; service is outstanding too.

South Delhi

Amarya Haveli

P-5 Hauz Khas Encl.(4175-9268). Visit www.amaryagroup.com. $$

The Amarya Haveli is owned by Alexandre Lieury and Mathieu Chanard, two Frenchmen who have made it their mission to combine Western comfort with oriental opulence. Each of the six rooms has a different theme and colour; the Jodhpuri Room is decorated entirely with blue motifs and designs from Jodhpur, while the Cochin Room is painted all in white with a golden Tree of Life emblazoned on the wall. There's a nice upstairs terrace, and a Japanese-themed common lounge and dining area. Located in a quiet, safe neighbourhood in south Delhi, it's the perfect distance from the noise of the city centre.

Bnineteen

B-19 Nizamuddin East (4182-5500). Visit www.bnineteen.com. $$

Bnineteen is luxury with a personalised touch from hosts Rajive and Janis. Rooms are decorated with objets d'art and antiques, the linen and upholstery are tasteful, and the bathrooms large. The terrace has great views of Humayun's Tomb, especially breathtaking at night when the monument is lit up. Meals on the candlelit terrace are delightful, as is the service at this stylish home away from home.

Bed & Breakfast at Eleven

11, Nizamuddin East (2435-1225). Visit www.elevendelhi.com. No credit cards. $$

A five-minute walk from Humayun's Tomb and a 10-minute drive from Central Delhi, this bed and breakfast occupies a colonial bungalow with a nice lawn and swing and a pleasant front patio. It's surrounded by greenery, lending a secluded, peaceful ambience. Decor is not particularly elegant, but all the rooms are comfortably furnished. What the Eleven lacks in high-end hotel luxury, it makes up for with simple domestic comfort.

Colonel's Retreat

D-418 Defence Colony (99997-20024). Visit www.colonels-retreat.com. No AmEx. $$
Located in the posh residential Defence Colony neighbourhood – loved by local bar-hoppers and expats alike – the Colonel's

rooms are simply furnished. Common areas comprise a dining room and a lounge with leather couch, armchairs, TV and a fully stocked bookshelf for guests who want to read up on Delhi or just lose themselves in a novel. There's no kitschy oriental opulence here – the simplicity of the Colonel's Retreat is a pleasure.

Inn at Delhi

South Delhi C-34 Anand Niketan (98681-40243). Visit www.innatdelhi.com. $$
Surrounded by parks and nestled in the pleasantly quiet and posh

Amarya Haveli

ESSENTIALS

The Manor

neighbourhood of Anand Niketan (also a diplomatic enclave), this inn is set in a three-storey mansion typical of the neighbourhood. It's run by Mr and Ms Subhash Chander, an amiable retired couple (he is a former professor, she used to be a doctor) who also live on the premises. They have taken pains to create a comfortable and pleasant space for guests and tailor the menu to suit their tastes. Bathrooms come with bathtubs; half of them have jacuzzis. Every room has a mini fridge, Indian paintings on the walls, embroidered pillows and bedspreads and cosy desk lamps,

all of which should make you feel right at home.

The Manor

77 Friends Colony West (2692-5151). Visit www.themanordelhi.com. $$$ With the mansions of media moguls, pharmaceutical millionaires and old-time oil industry executives as its neighbours, the Manor certainly has an impeccable address. Some of these magnates can occasionally be found on the hotel's large lawn, having discreet meetings or simply enjoying a cocktail or two. The hotel has been around since the 1950s, but it has had an international-style makeover: The decor is minimal with just a flash of marigold. The 15 rooms are spacious, with wood-panelled floors and walls, large beds and writing tables. Make sure to eat at the restaurant, Indian Accent (p169), which has been winning enthusiastic reviews for its Indian-fusion cuisine. The menu includes the likes of tamarind-glazed lamb shanks, masala morels and Indian breads stuffed with mushrooms and drizzled with truffle oil.

Trinity Art Hotel

E -147, Saket, near PVR Anupam (4056-8989). $$$

Have you ever enjoyed a gallery so much you wished you could stay? Now you can do just that. The Trinity Art Hotel, run by Sheetal Bawa Singh and her husband, has the dual intention of being a chic, boutique hotel and of exhibiting the art of Hemi Bawa, who is Singh's mother. The white walls and sparse furnishings give the Art Hotel the convincing air of a gallery, and keep the paintings at the centre of attention. The rooms are studio-size and there's room service from restaurants in the Saket area.

Thikana

A-7 Gulmohar Park (4604-1569). Visit www.thikanadelhi.com. No AmEx. $$

Tiny photos of four generations of the family that runs this airy B&B hang from twigs stuck into a glass bowl in the dining room: just Sheetal and Atul Bhalla's many little touches. There's also tasteful Indian art on the walls and traditional home-cooked meals available on request. Though Thikana is located on a busy street, its eight rooms are strangely quiet. They're also elegantly furnished, with large beds and inviting armchairs. Bathrooms are spotless, and are supplied with handmade soap. The living room has TV, free internet and photocopying facilities. Thikana is around a 25-minute taxi ride away from the Connaught Place tourist hub, and is popular with NGO workers and foreign correspondents. Guests are made to feel welcome.

West Delhi

Shanti Home

A-1/300 Janakpuri (4157-3366). Visit www.shantihome.com. No AmEx. $$

Close to the international airport and five minutes from the closest Metro station, this boutique hotel is a bit far from the main sights, though some visitors may not think that a bad thing.

The decor is a fusion of styles, but high-backed carved benches, urulis of flower petals, statues of Ganesha other Hindu figurines and oriental carpets adorn the foyer and common areas. Wi-Fi and breakfast are included in the room charge, and there's also a lounge with desktop computer. "Shanti" means inner peace in Hindi, and the hotel makes every effort to help their guests attain such a state of bliss. On the rooftop is a 24-hour restaurant and bar.

ESSENTIALS

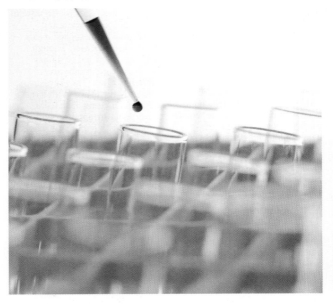

Medical Tourism

People fly in from around the world to receive medical treatment in India. For most, it's cheaper (approximately a tenth of costs in Western Europe); for some, there are facilities that aren't available in their home countries. The medical tourism business is very controversial – enough good Indian doctors leave the country anyway, and it's hard for some to accept visitors occupying the ones who have stayed. Yet the industry is still an unstructured one, and it's growing by leaps and bounds. By 2012, it's expected that it will be an $8.5 billion industry.

People visit India for a range of procedures, from life-saving cardiac surgery or bone-marrow transplants, to liposuction, tooth-whitening and fitting dentures. Many hospitals have offices to assist international patients. Also, a new breed of travel agent now specialises in medical tourism, arranging everything for patients: airport pick-ups, interpreting Indian languages, arranging sightseeing and spa trips. Some even operate concierge services, which recommend restaurants, arrange cars and tell you how much to tip. Once recovered, many visitors like to visit the Taj Mahal and go shopping.

Tips

Check accreditation

You may want to select a hospital with recognised accreditation. The Joint Commission International (www.jointcommissioninternational.org) accredits healthcare organisations, though its list of reliable hospitals in Delhi is far from comprehensive. Other certifications like the ISO-9000 can also be a good indicator of quality care. You can ask for a doctors' details in advance.

Get a reputed agent: Some visitors prefer to work with a medical tourism agent to select the right hospital. These agencies also offer travel bookings and other concierge services.

Sahara Medical Tourism, *DLF Infinity Towers, Tower A, 2nd Floor, Gurgaon (0124-4318888). Contact Vishal Laroia (98104-95927).*

Get feedback: Talk to local acquaintances about a hospital's reputation. Apart from quality of care availble, it's worth asking about the total cost involved. Many private hospitals are notorious for inflating their diagnostic and clinical costs.

JCI-accredited hospitals

Fortis Escorts Heart Institute
Okhla Road, near New Friends Colony (4713-5000 or email contactus.escorts@fortishealth-care.com).

Indraprastha Apollo Hospital
Sarita Vihar, Delhi-Mathura Road (99582-90344, 2692-5858, 2692-5801 extn. 1849 or email banasree_b@apollohospitals.com).

Moolchand Hospital
Lajpat Nagar III, next to Defence Colony flyover (99589-97293 or email clinic@moolchand-healthcare.com).

Moolchand Hospital

Major Dhyan Chand Stadium

The Commonwealth Games 2010

For better or for worse, international athletic events in Delhi have always meant the city's reinvention. Around the 1951 Asian Games, the 1982 Asian Games and now the 2010 Commonwealth Games, city authorities have built new infrastructure, "beautified" the city centre, attempted to eject everything unsightly from beggars to horse-drawn tonga carriages, and spun a new image of Delhi as "a world-class city". The city has been through five years of turbulent transformation getting ready for the Games. Towards the end, however, official preparations became diverted into massive corruption. It's unfortunate but true that organisers were so intent on winning over delegates and visitors, they forgot to win over Delhi's residents. You won't find much love for Shera, the Games' sneaker-wearing tiger mascot, either.

None of this has to detract from the quality and the excitement of the 17 athletic competitions themselves. The para-sports component for the Games, for disabled athletes, will account for 45 medals – a gold, silver and a bronze in each event. The 13 competition venues have been listed in the Delhi by Area chapters (highlighted as stadia under Sights & Museums) and marked on the area maps. The only exception is the Noida Expressway, the location for the cycling time trials (an unticketed event).

Tickets Tickets are available for purchase city-wide at branches of the Central Bank of India, and outlets of Hero Honda and the FastTrax fast-food chain. They can also be purchased online at www.tickets.cwgdelhi2010.org or purchsed over the toll-free numbers 1800-1021294 or 1800-2001294 (payment by credit card). Finally, you can also buy tickets at the box office at the event venue.

Event schedule

Event		Venue	Event dates
Opening Ceremony		JN Stadium	3 Oct 2010
Closing Ceremony		JN Stadium	14 Oct 2010
Aquatics	Diving	Dr SPM Swimming Complex	10-13 Oct 2010
	Swimming		4-9 Oct 2010
	Synchronised Swimming		6-7 Oct 2010
Archery		Yamuna Sports Complex	4-10 Oct 2010
Athletics	Track & Field	JN Stadium	6-12 Oct 2010
	Marathon	JN Stadium/Marathon Course	14 Oct 2010
	Walk		09 Oct 2010
Badminton		Siri Fort Sports Complex	4-14 Oct 2010
Boxing		Talkatora Indoor Stadium	5-11, 13 Oct 2010
Cycling	Track	IG Sports Complex	5-8 Oct 2010
	Road Mass Start		10 Oct 2010
	Road Time Trials	Noida Highway Express Rd	13 Oct 2010
Gymnastics	Artistic	IG Sports Complex	4-8 Oct 2010
	Rhythmic		12-14 Oct 2010
Hockey		Maj. Dhyan Chand National Stadium	4-14 Oct 2010
Lawn Bowls		JN Sports Complex	4-13 Oct 2010
Netball		Thyagaraj Sports Complex	4-12, 14 Oct 2010
Rugby Sevens		Delhi University	11-12 Oct 2010
Shooting	Clay Target	Dr Karni Singh Shooting Range	6-13 Oct 2010
	Full Bore	CRPF Campus, Kadarpur	9-13 Oct 2010
	Pistol and Small Bore	Dr Karni Singh Shooting Range	5-13 Oct 2010
Squash		Siri Fort Sports Complex	4-13 Oct 2010
Table Tennis		Yamuna Sports Complex	4-14 Oct 2010
Tennis		RK Khanna Tennis Stadium	4-10 Oct 2010
Weightlifting		JN Sports Complex	4-12 Oct 2010
Wrestling		IG Sports Complex	5-10 Oct 2010

ESSENTIALS

Getting around

Climate

Anybody arriving in Delhi knows what to expect: heat. For about five months of the year (from late March to late August) Delhi warms up like a baker's oven. Temperatures soar to over 45 degrees Celsius in May and June. The summer months are best avoided, especially if you're not accustomed to intense heat. The city begins to cool with the monsoons between July and September. The monsoon is unpredictable, but once it rains it pours, and the formerly desert-dry city floods. Winters are short but the city gets surprisingly chilly and foggy in December and January. Fog interferes with late night and early morning flights through December and January. The short and celebrated spring (February and March) and autumn (October and November) seasons are the most pleasant, with temperatures between 11 and 27 degrees Celsius.

Getting in

Indira Gandhi International Airport, on the city's south-western fringe, is Delhi's main arrival point. The integrated Terminal 3 building, which opened in July 2010, is the largest passenger terminal in the world after Dubai and Beijing.

The best way to get from the airport to town is to make prior transport arrangements with your hotel. You can also use private "radio taxis", which have online booking, though you'll need an Indian cellphone or landline number to book one. They will wait in the VIP car park opposite Arrivals. A trip to hotels in north Delhi (such as the Hotel Broadway and Oberoi Maidens) should cost around ₹ 500.

Alternatively, you can hire a reliable, inexpensive taxi at the prepaid taxi booth managed by the Delhi Police. You have to give the receipt to the driver once you reach your destination. Tipping taxi drivers is not mandatory anywhere in India, but is always appreciated. It is also possible to take the Metro airport link into town. Ignore taxi touts.

During the peak of winter (Dec-Jan), Delhi is often blanketed in opaque fog, reducing visibility considerably. Night and morning flights are often diverted or cancelled, so book afternoon flights or allow for delays.

Getting out of Delhi

Delhi Tourism has an office at Baba Kharak Singh Marg. Its travel division, responsibile for organising car hire, guided tours and so on, is in Connaught Place. *Coffee Home, Baba Kharak Singh*

Marg (2336-5358), Mon-Sat 10am-7pm. N-36 Bombay Life Building, Middle Circle, Connaught Place (2331-5322). Mon-Sat 10am-7pm. ⊖ Rajiv Chowk. Call the tourist helpline at (2336-5358, 2336-3607) or visit www.delhitourism.nic.in.

By bus

While not as comfortable as trains, buses are the only choice for some destinations, like the hill-states of Uttarakhand and Himachal Pradesh. Delhi has three major inter-state bus terminals (ISBT). The Delhi Transport Corporation is the major operator, but state transport corporations run their own fleets. So do private operators.

Kashmere Gate ISBT (also called Maharana Pratap Bus Terminal) is the largest terminal. Sarai Kale Khan ISBT is next to Hazrat Nizamuddin railway station, and Anand Vihar ISBT is east of the Yamuna. Buses to Rajasthan depart and arrive at **Bikaner House** near India Gate. It is best to buy a ticket at least 40 minutes before your departure to avoid long queues at the counter. From **Himachal Bhavan**, the Himachal Pradesh state tourism corporation runs buses to Shimla, Dharamshala, Manali and other Himalayan destinations.
Bikaner House *Pandara Road, India Gate (2338-3469).*
Himachal Bhavan *27 Sikandra Road, Mandi House (2371-6126).* ⊖ *Mandi House*

By train

Out of the city's four railway stations, Old Delhi, New Delhi and Hazrat Nizamuddin are the only ones you're likely to be using. If you're heading to Varanasi however, you'll need to use the Anand Vihar station. Delhi Junction and New Delhi Railway Station are connected by Metro Line 2, while Anand Vihar is on the Metro's Line 3. Once you've bought a train ticket, all you need to do is go to the compartment marked on your ticket. Booking opens 90 days ahead of travel and seats and berths on popular routes like Delhi-Shimla are often booked well in advance during peak season (Nov-Mar). However, a small "tourist quota" of seats is held for foreign nationals. These must be bought from the special tourist reservation offices or counters at the New Delhi station (on the first floor) and are not available online. A passport is required as proof of nationality. US dollars, pounds sterling and euros are accepted. If you're paying in rupees you'll need to show a foreign exchange receipt or ATM slip.

You don't need a boarding pass on the train, which is one method scamsters use to rip travellers off. The best way to get train tickets is the Indian Railways website (www.irctc.co.in). Travel sites such as www.makemytrip.com are also reliable . If you're doing a lot of travelling you can also buy an Indrail pass (from the same

ESSENTIALS

Getting around

counter as the foreigners' quota tickets), which offers unlimited rail travel across India for upto 90 days.

Classes of service

Long-distance trains will have some or all of the following classes depending on the route: AC first class (**1A**) is the most expensive, with fares comparable to airfare. Passengers have a comfortable sleeping cubicle (two people in each) with a door that can be locked. Then come the AC two-tier (**2A**) and AC three-tier (**3A**) classes. All three are air-conditioned and have tinted windows and padded berths. Blankets, bed sheets and pillows are provided, the compartment doors are secured at night and attendants are available. Some trains also have a non-air-conditioned first class (**FC**), the most pleasant in good weather. The sleeper class (**SL**) is not air-conditioned and is three-tier. Trains travelling shorter distances have some or both of these classes: the air-conditioned chair car (**CC**), which has comfortable individual seats that recline, and second seating (**SS**), which may be anything from a wooden seat to a narrow padded bench to be shared by three people.

Getting around Delhi

Getting around the city is usually an adventure. Traffic tends to be heavy, but taxi and autorickshaws are easy to find. While it still doesn't cover the whole city, the new Metro is a safe and quick way to get around – especially to travel long distances when the traffic is ugly. Cycle-rickshaws in congested areas are a good option; fix a price and hop on.

Auto-rickshaws

Three-wheeled, open-sided "autos" are quintessential Delhi transport, and locals love them as much as they're exasperated by them. Prepare to feel both ways. According to their permit rules, autos should take you wherever you want, charging you by meter, which costs ₹ 19 for the first two kilometres; add ₹ 6.50 per kilometre after that. If a driver has an out-dated meter, he will be carrying a fare chart that you can ask to see. If he indicates that his meter isn't working, agree on the price in advance.

Bus

Locals navigate the bus routes through a form of complex social memory, which is not easy to plug into. But the buses are safe, cheap and interesting ways to get around. Delhi Transport Corporation buses charge ₹ 5-20 a ticket within the city. Use the new low-floor buses, they're more comfortable, especially the red air-con option (prices range between ₹ 10-25 for adults and ₹ 5-13 for kids).

Cycle-rickshaws

They don't use meters at all, so establish a price before getting on.

Thirty rupees is reasonable for most journeys of a kilometre or two. Cycle-rickshaws are common in Old Delhi, Delhi University's north campus, most of west and east Delhi and some areas of south Delhi, Gurgaon and Noida.

Taxis

Most public taxis are the old but reliable Ambassadors with a distinctive black-and-yellow paint job, which are usually not air-conditioned. Fares begin at ₹ 20 for the first kilometre, add ₹ 11 per kilometre after that. Most trips around the city should cost around ₹ 500, while a trip to the airport costs around ₹ 300. An eight-hour hire should cost around ₹ 800. You can't just hail a cab anywhere (except at railway stations), but most neighbourhoods have stands where you can get one (ask a local for the number). If you take a taxi from a local stand, negotiate the price in advance. Rental rates vary depending on the size and model of the car, whether it's air-conditioned or not, and whether the car will be used within the city or outside the city limits. Prices range from ₹ 6 to ₹ 20 per kilometre, with a minimum charge of 200 to 250 kilometres per day. The compact Indica taxi (from Tata Motors) is invariably the cheapest. For longer drives, an SUV is better. Private radio taxis charge ₹ 15 per kilometre. These taxis are air-conditioned and can be called upon 24 hours a day.

Carzonrent *Call (4184-1212) or book online at ww.carzonrent.com.*
Delhi Cabs *Call (4433-3222).*
Easy Cabs *Call (4343-4343).*
Orix Cabs *Call (4562-8200 or 2591-7441) for New Delhi and (0124-3014700) for Gurgaon*
Mega Cab *Call (4141-4141) or book online at www.megacabs.com.*
Meru Cabs *Call (4422-4422) or book online at www.merucabs.com.*
Quick Cabs *Call (4533-3333) or visit www.quickcabs.in.*
Routes Dial-a-Cab *Call (4440-4440).*

Metro

It is almost unanimous among Dilliwalas that the Delhi Metro Rail is the best thing to happen to this city in centuries. Wherever appropriate, we've indicated the nearest convenient Metro stop with a ⊖ for all our listings. The Metro lets you cut right through the city's vast sprawl and rush-hour traffic; it connects the heart of the city, Connaught Place (⊖ Rajiv Chowk) to all the cardinal points of the National Capital Region. Many lines run on elevated tracks, so there's a good view to boot. And did we mention the air-conditioning?

Fares range from ₹ 8 to ₹ 30. Buy a token to your destination and change lines as necessary, depositing the token in the exit turnstile at your final destination. Metro tokens can be used only for a one-way journey, so you'll need to buy another token for the return journey. You can also buy a

Smart Card for ₹ 50 to avoid the queues at the token counter. There is also a Tourist Card that allows you unlimited use for ₹ 100 (one-day validity) or ₹ 250 (three days).

Line 2 (usually the "Yellow Line") will be the most useful, as it reaches into North Delhi (Coronation Park, Kashmere Gate ISBT), Old Delhi (Red Fort, the Jama Masjid) and through Connaught Place down into South Delhi (Hauz Khas, the Qutab Complex) and Gurgaon.

Line 3 (usually the "Blue Line") is handy for visiting the Akshardham Temple to the east and the backpacker haunts of Paharganj.

Language

Almost all Dilliwalas speak Hindi or Hindi and an additional regional language. Quite a few – including many shopkeepers and auto- and taxi drivers – will be able to communicate in English. Most educated people you meet will speak a flowing mix of Hindi and English, which allows visitors to pick up Hindi quicker. Be brave and use our phrasebook (p227).

Women's safety

This has long been Delhi's weak-point. If you are a woman moving through the city, be prepared for stares, provocative remarks and the likelihood of some groping in crowds. Ask bystanders for help if it gets bad. If you're arriving at night, make sure to arrange for safe transport (see Getting into town). Depending on what part of

the city you're visiting, it may be wise to dress conservatively (no bare arms or legs). In most parts of Old Delhi this is a good idea, in most of south Delhi it isn't necessary. Police patrol cars (called PCR vans) are parked on every major intersection. Dial 100 in case of emergencies. Carry your cash, passport, and cards in a secure money belt, with only enough cash for one day at a time in your wallet or any other accessible place.

Swimming in lakes and rivers is not allowed. Instead, look for a hotel with a swimming pool, since many offer day passes, or go for a walk in one of the many parks.

Power supply

Power in India is supplied at 220-250 v/ac at 50 hz.

Internet

Internet cafés can be found all over the city.

Cash machines

Automatic teller machines with 24-hour access that accept both Visa and MasterCard are easily found around markets, banks and malls. But you don't want to end up in Old Delhi or North Delhi looking for one.

Banking hours

India's banking hours are Monday to Friday from 9am to 6pm and Saturday from 9.30am to noon.

Smoking

India follows strict no-smoking

ESSENTIALS

regulations. Smoking is not permitted in any public office space, airport or on public transport. Restaurants and hotels do not permit smoking in their dining areas. Smokers can look out for restaurants or bars with balconies. Based on a policy by the Organising Committee of the Commonwealth Games, all Games competition venues are strictly non-smoking, except in designated outdoor areas.

Airline information

Indian Airlines India's national carrier. *Call (1800-227722) or visit www.indian-airlines.nic.in.* Numerous private airlines also fly all over the country and to select international destinations. All are fairly reliable, and prices vary.
Kingfisher *Call (1800-2093030) or visit www.flykingfisher.com.*
Jet Airways *Call (1800-225522) or visit www.jetairways.com.*
Jet Lite *Call (1800-223020) or visit www.jetairways.com.*
SpiceJet *Call (98718-03333) or visit www.spicejet.com.*
GoAir *Call (1800-222111) or visit www.goair.in.*
Indigo *Call (99103-83838) or visit www.goindigo.in.*

Calling within India (STD)

Delhi's area code is 011. When dialing from Delhi to areas outside the city, prefix the area code of the place you are calling before the local number. For example: Noida 0120, Gurgaon 0124, Mumbai 022, Bangalore 080 Chennai 044, Kolkata 033.

Calling overseas

The outgoing international code is 00, followed by the country code and the area code. For example, to call London dial 00 (international code), 44 (country code), 20 (area code) and then the local number.

Calling Delhi from overseas

International access codes vary depending on the country you're calling from. However, in general, to call Delhi from overseas dial 0091 (India code) 11 (Delhi code), and then the local eight-digit landline number. To reach a cellphone, dial 0091 and then the ten-digit mobile number.

Tips

● When visiting the crowded lanes of Old Delhi carry only what you need, in your front pocket or close to your body. Pickpocketing is not uncommon in congested areas like Chandni Chowk or Palika Bazar.
● Beware of tourist traps. The most common are agencies that pretend to be government-run tourist offices. It's hard to tell them apart from the real thing, so it's best to take the recommendations of a hotel or reputable agent. Anything that seems too good to be true usually is.
● Again: between mid-December and the end of January, Delhi sees thick fog that hampers flight arrivals and departures. Try to book yourself on afternoon flights, but do recheck with the airline for any delays.

Vocabulary

Useful phrases

Hello Namaste; **How are you** Aap kaise hai; **Sorry / excuse me** Maaf keejiye; **See you later** Phir milenge; **Thank you** Dhanyavaad; **Yes/no** Haan / Nahi; **I don't know** Mujhe nahi pata; **Who? / what?** kaun? / kya?; **Where? / why?** kahan? / kyon?; **How much?** (cost) Kitne ka? **How many?** Kitne?

Basic conversation

Do you know English? Aapko English aati hai? **I don't know Hindi** Mujhe Hindi nahi aati. **How are you?** Aap kaise hai? **My name is...** Mera naam hai... **What is your name?** Apka naam kya hai? **What do you do?** Aap kya kartein hai? **Where is ...?** .... kidhar hai? **It's too much** Bahut zyada hai. **It's not enough.** Bahut kum hai. **Please come here.** Idhar aiye. **Please go.** Chale jayiye. **Now** Abhi. **Later.** Baad mein. **Where is the restroom?** Toilet kidhar hai? **Do you have...?** Aapke pas...hai? **Less spice:** Mirchi kum; **Less sugar:** Cheeni kum.

General glossary

Auto: Motorised three-wheeler; **Baoli:** Stepwell; **Baagh:** Garden; **Bhai:** Brother; **Chemist:** Pharmacy; **Dargah:** Shrine at a Sufi saint's grave; **Darwaza:** Gate/door; **Dilliwala:** Delhi resident; **Din:** Day; **Dost:** Friend; **Gali:** Lane; **Girijaghar:** Church; **Gurdwara:** Sikh temple; **Hafta:** Week; **Haveli:** Mansion; **Kal:** Tomorrow / yesterday; **Mandir:** Temple; **Masjid:** Mosque; **Mazaar:** Tomb; **Minar:** Minaret; **Pir:** Sufi saint; **Prasad:** Offerings blessed at temples, often sweets; **Qila:** Fort; **Raat:** Night; **Sarai:** Historical travellers' rest-stop; **Lakh:** Hundred thousand; **Crore:** Ten million.

Numbers

1: aik; **2:** do; **3:** teen; **4:** chaar; **5:** paanch; **6:** chey; **7:** saath; **8:** aath; **9:** naw; **10:** dus; **20:** bees; **50:** pachaas; **100:** saw; **500:** paanch saw; **1000:** hazaar; **1,00,000:** lakh; **1,00,00,000:** crore

Food glossary

Aloo: Potato; **Adrak:** Ginger; **Anda:** Egg; **Angoor:** Grapes; **Banta:** Fizzy lemonade; **Biryani:** Slow-cooked meat pilaf; **Buff:** Buffalo meat substituting beef; **Chai:** Tea; **Chaat:** Savoury street-side snacks; **Cheeni:** Sugar; **Chawal:** Rice; **Dahi:** Yoghurt; **Dhaba:** Small restaurants serving local food; **Double roti:** Bread; **Garam:** Hot; **Ghee:** Clarified butter; **Karara:** Crisp; **Keema:** Minced meat; **Kela:** Banana; **Makhan:** Butter; **Meetha:** Sweet; **Naan:** Leavened flat bread; **Namak:** Salt; **Nimbu:** Lemon; **Nimbupaani:** Lemonade; **Nimbu soda:** Fresh lime soda; **Paan:** Betel leaf; **Paani:** Water; **Paneer:** Fresh cottage cheese; **Parantha:** Shallow-fried flat breads; **Masala:** Spice; **Moongphalli:** Peanut; **Phirni:** Creamy rice pudding; **Raita:** Yoghurt relish; **Roti/chapati:** Unleavened flat bread; **Saag:** Cooked spinach or other greens; **Seb:** Apple; **Santara:** (fruit) Orange; **Saunf:** Aniseed; **Shakahari:** Vegetarian; **Supari:** Areca nut; **Teekha:** Spicy; **Thanda:** Cold; **Thaali:** Serving of multiple dishes that make for a complete meal.

Directions

Right: Daayein; **Left:** Baayein; **Up:** Upar; **Down:** Neeche; **Near:** Pass mein; **Far:** Duur; **Inside:** Andar; **Outside:** Bahar; **Here:** Idhar; **There:** Udhar.

Index

Index

ESSENTIALS